First
Dictionary

Schofield&Sims

Published by Schofield and Sims Limited, Dogley Mill, Fenay Bridge, Huddersfield HD8 0NQ, UK
Telephone 01484 607080

www.schofieldandsims.co.uk

Original edition first published in 1989
This revised and updated edition first published in 2009
Second impression 2013

Editorial project management by
Carolyn Richardson Publishing Services (cr@publiserve.co.uk)

Design by **Oxford Designers & Illustrators**

Printed in the UK by **Wyndeham Gait Ltd**, Grimsby, Lincolnshire

ISBN 978 0 7217 1141 6

Contents

What is a dictionary?

A dictionary is a reference book.

You can use it when you are reading or writing.

You can use it to look things up.

It contains words arranged in alphabetical order.

These words are called headwords.

A dictionary tells you the meaning of every headword.

A dictionary also shows you how to spell words.

What is special about this dictionary?

This dictionary gives you some extra help:

➲ It shows you **how to say** some words. For example, it tells you how to say the word 'use' when it means 'to do something with'. It tells you to say 'yooz'.

➲ It shows you how some words are **shortened**. For example, 'vegetables' is sometimes shortened to 'veg'.

➲ It gives you the **plurals** of words. 'Plural' means 'more than one'. For example, beside the word 'van' is the plural 'vans'.

➲ It gives you **other word forms** too.

Here is one example. After the word 'vanish' are the words 'vanishes, vanishing, vanished'. You would use these words in different sentences. You could say 'He vanishes', 'He was vanishing' or 'He vanished'.

Here is another example. After the word 'vain' are the words 'vainer, vainest'. You would use these words if you wanted to say how vain two people are. For example, you might want to compare two characters in a story.

Now look at the diagram opposite.

Read all the labels.

They will help you learn how to use this book.

How to use this book

The words in dark blue are called **headwords**. They are shown in alphabetical order.

The **guide word** in this corner tells you the **first** word on this page. The guide words help you to find your way round the book.

The big red letters show the start of a **new section**.

There is a word next to some of the headwords. This is the **plural**. The plural is the word you use for more than one of these things.

The **guide word** in this corner tells you the **last** word on this page. The **guide words** help you to find your way round the book.

The black words under the headwords are called **definitions**. They tell you what the word means.

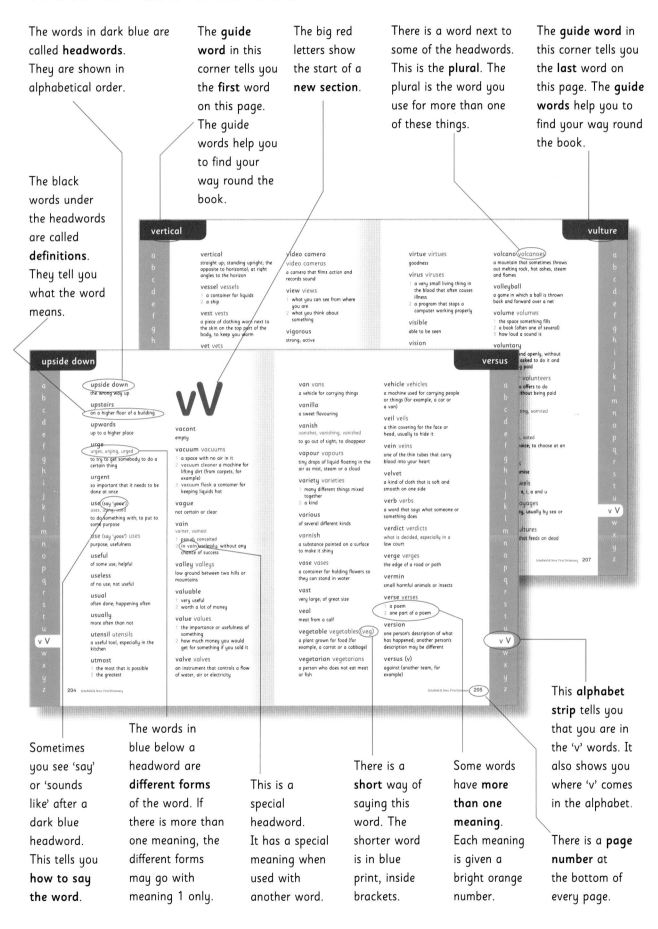

vertical
vertical
straight up; standing upright; the opposite to horizontal; at right angles to the horizon

vessel vessels
1 a container for liquids
2 a ship

vest vests
a piece of clothing worn next to the skin on the top part of the body, to keep you warm

vet vets

video camera
video cameras
a camera that films action and records sound

view views
1 what you can see from where you are
2 what you think about something

vigorous
strong, active

virtue virtues
goodness

virus viruses
1 a very small living thing in the blood that often causes illness
2 a program that stops a computer working properly

visible
able to be seen

vision

volcano volcanoes
a mountain that sometimes throws out melting rock, hot ashes, steam and flames

volleyball
a game in which a ball is thrown back and forward over a net

volume volumes
1 the space something fills
2 a book (often one of several)
3 how loud a sound is

voluntary

vulture

upside down
upside down
the wrong way up

upstairs
on a higher floor of a building

upwards
up to a higher place

urge
urges, urging, urged
to try to get somebody to do a certain thing

urgent
so important that it needs to be done at once

use (say 'yooz')
uses, using, used
to do something with; to put to some purpose

use (say 'yoos') uses
purpose; usefulness

useful
of some use; helpful

useless
of no use; not useful

usual
often done; happening often

usually
more often than not

utensil utensils
a useful tool, especially in the kitchen

utmost
1 the most that is possible
2 the greatest

vV

vacant
empty

vacuum vacuums
1 a space with no air in it
2 vacuum cleaner a machine for lifting dirt (from carpets, for example)
3 vacuum flask a container for keeping liquids hot

vague
not certain or clear

vain
vainer, vainest
1 proud, conceited
2 in vain uselessly; without any chance of success

valley valleys
low ground between two hills or mountains

valuable
1 very useful
2 worth a lot of money

value values
1 the importance or usefulness of something
2 how much money you would get for something if you sold it

valve valves
an instrument that controls a flow of water, air or electricity

van vans
a vehicle for carrying things

vanilla
a sweet flavouring

vanish
vanishes, vanishing, vanished
to go out of sight; to disappear

vapour vapours
tiny drops of liquid floating in the air as mist, steam or a cloud

variety varieties
1 many different things mixed together
2 a kind

various
of several different kinds

varnish
a substance painted on a surface to make it shiny

vase vases
a container for holding flowers so they can stand in water

vast
very large; of great size

veal
meat from a calf

vegetable vegetables (veg)
a plant grown for food (for example, a carrot or a cabbage)

vegetarian vegetarians
a person who does not eat meat or fish

vehicle vehicles
a machine used for carrying people or things (for example, a car or a van)

veil veils
a thin covering for the face or head, usually to hide it

vein veins
one of the thin tubes that carry blood into your heart

velvet
a kind of cloth that is soft and smooth on one side

verb verbs
a word that says what someone or something does

verdict verdicts
what is decided, especially in a law court

verge verges
the edge of a road or path

vermin
small harmful animals or insects

verse verses
1 a poem
2 one part of a poem

version
one person's description of what has happened; another person's description may be different

versus (v)
against (another team, for example)

versus
...nd openly, without ...asked to do it and ...g paid

...volunteers
...a offers to do ...ithout being paid

...ting, vomited

...voted
...hoice; to choose at an

...mise

...wels
...e, i, o and u

...oyages
...ey, usually by sea or

...ultures
...that feeds on dead

Sometimes you see 'say' or 'sounds like' after a dark blue headword. This tells you **how to say the word**.

The words in blue below a headword are **different forms** of the word. If there is more than one meaning, the different forms may go with meaning 1 only.

This is a special headword. It has a special meaning when used with another word.

There is a **short** way of saying this word. The shorter word is in blue print, inside brackets.

Some words have **more than one meaning**. Each meaning is given a bright orange number.

This **alphabet strip** tells you that you are in the 'v' words. It also shows you where 'v' comes in the alphabet.

There is a **page number** at the bottom of every page.

a A

b c d e f g h i j k l m n o p q r s t u v w x y z

aA

abandon
abandons, abandoning, abandoned

1 to leave, often for ever
2 to give up

abbreviation
abbreviations

a shortened word, for example
Dr (Doctor), Rd (Road)

ability abilities

being able to do things

able
abler, ablest

having the skill to do something

aboard

on a ship or an aircraft

abolish
abolishes, abolishing, abolished

to get rid of something

about

1 concerning; to do with
2 nearly

above

1 over
2 higher than

abroad

in or to another country

abruptly
very quickly; suddenly

absent
not here; not present

absolutely
completely; quite so

absurd
silly; without any sense

accent accents
the way people speak a
language

accept
accepts, accepting, accepted

to take something that is offered
or given

accident accidents
something bad that happens
by chance

accommodation
somewhere to live or stay

accompany
accompanies, accompanying,
accompanied

1 to go with
2 to play a musical instrument
along with

account accounts
1 a bill showing money owed
2 a statement of money received
and spent (for example, a bank
statement)
3 a piece of writing that describes
an event
4 to account for to explain how
something happened

accurate

exactly right

accuse

accuses, accusing, accused

to say that someone has done something wrong

ace aces

1 a high-scoring playing card
2 really good

ache aches

a pain in some part of the body

achieve

achieves, achieving, achieved

to manage to do something, usually with effort

acid acids

a strong liquid that can burn things

acorn acorns

the fruit of the oak tree

acquaintance

acquaintances

a person you know slightly but not very well

acrobat acrobats

a person who does leaping and balancing tricks

across

1 from one side to the other
2 on the other side of something

act

acts, acting, acted

1 to do something
2 a part of a play
3 to perform on stage

action actions

1 a movement of your body
2 something done for a particular purpose

active

lively

actor actors

a man or woman who performs in a play, a film or on television

actual

real; existing

add

adds, adding, added

1 to find the total of two or more numbers (+)
2 to put together with something else

adder adders

a small poisonous snake

address addresses

1 the building, street and town where you live
2 to write to; to speak to

adjective adjectives

a word that describes something

admiral admirals

the most important officer in the navy

admire

admires, admiring, admired

to think well of someone or something

b
c
d
e
f
g
h
i
j
k
l
m
n
o
p
q
r
s
t
u
v
w
x
y
z

admission

1 being allowed into a place or group
2 what you pay for this

admit

admits, admitting, admitted

1 to agree that something has happened or is true
2 to allow someone or something to enter

adolescent adolescents

someone who is half way between being a child and an adult; a teenager

adopt

adopts, adopting, adopted

to take into your family and care for as your own

adore

adores, adoring, adored

to love very much

adrift

drifting on water in a boat or on a raft

adult adults

a grown-up person

advance

advances, advancing, advanced

to move forward

adventure adventures

an exciting happening

adverb adverbs

a word that tells you more about a verb

advertise

advertises, advertising, advertised

to make well-known (in a newspaper, for example)

advertisement (advert) advertisements (adverts)

a short performance or piece of writing that aims to make something well-known

advice

what you say to someone to help them decide what they should do

advise

advises, advising, advised

to tell other people what you think they should do

aerial aerials

a wire that sends out or picks up radio or television signals

aeroplane (plane) aeroplanes (planes)

a flying machine

affect

affects, affecting, affected

to cause a change in things or people

affectionate

showing love for something or somebody

afford

affords, affording, afforded

to be able to pay for

afraid

frightened; full of fear

after

behind; following

afternoon afternoons

the time of the day between morning and evening

afterwards

later

again

once more

against

1 on the opposite side to (in a game, for example)
2 next to and touching someone or something

age ages

1 how old you are
2 a special time in history, such as the Stone Age

ago

in the past

agony agonies

great pain

agree

agrees, agreeing, agreed

1 to think the same
2 **agree to** to accept that something will happen or that you will do something

aground

caught in sand or rocks in shallow water (especially of a boat)

ahead

in front

aid

aids, aiding, aided

1 to help
2 help

aim

aims, aiming, aimed

1 to point at
2 to try to do something

aimless

without any purpose

air

1 the gas that you breathe
2 to make clothes or a room fresh by letting air into them

aircraft aircraft

an aeroplane (plane)

airport airports

a place where aircraft land and take off

ajar

partly open

alarm alarms

1 a warning bell or other sound
2 a sudden fright

album albums

1 a collection of things kept in a book (for example, photographs or stamps)
2 a collection of music on a CD

alert

ready to act; wide awake

alien aliens

someone from another planet

a A
b
c
d
e
f
g
h
i
j
k
l
m
n
o
p
q
r
s
t
u
v
w
x
y
z

alike

the same; similar

alive

living; not dead

all

everything; everyone

allergic (say 'aller**jick**')

made ill by certain foods or things

alley alleys

a very narrow street between buildings

alligator alligators

a kind of reptile that is like a crocodile

allow

allows, allowing, allowed

to let someone do something

ally allies

someone who is on your side (in an argument, for example)

almond (say '**aa**mond')

almonds

a kind of nut that is often used in cooking

almost

nearly; not quite

alone

by yourself

along

from one end to the other

aloud

in a voice loud enough to be heard

alphabet alphabets

the letters of a language in a fixed order (for example, a, b, c)

already

1 by this time
2 before this

also

as well

altar altars

the holy table in church

alter

alters, altering, altered

to make something different in some way; to change

although

even if; though

altogether

counting everybody or everything

aluminium

a light silvery-coloured metal

always

for ever; at all times

a.m.

the time between midnight and noon; morning

amazing

very surprising

ambition ambitions

the desire to achieve or to do something

ambitious

keen to do well at something

amble
ambles, ambling, ambled
to walk slowly; to stroll

ambulance ambulances
a van that is used to carry people who are ill or have been hurt

amen
the ending of a prayer

amid
in the middle of

among
in the middle of; surrounded by

amount amounts
a quantity; a sum

amphibian amphibians
an animal that can live in water and on land

amuse
amuses, amusing, amused
to make someone laugh or smile

ancestor ancestors
someone in your family who lived before you were born

anchor anchors
a heavy weight that is dropped to the bottom of the sea when the crew wants a ship to stop

ancient (say 'ainshunt')
very old; belonging to long ago

angel angels
someone who is believed to bring messages from God

angle angles
the space between two straight lines that meet at a point

angry
angrier, angriest
in a bad temper

animal animals
a living creature that can move

ankle ankles
the joint between the leg and the foot

anniversary anniversaries
the same date each year when something happened in the past

announce
announces, announcing, announced
to say things to a lot of people

annoy
annoys, annoying, annoyed
to make somebody upset or angry

annual
1 happening every year
2 a book that comes out each year

another
1 one more
2 a different one

answer answers
what you say or write when asked a question

ant ants
a tiny insect that lives in large groups

a A
b
c
d
e
f
g
h
i
j
k
l
m
n
o
p
q
r
s
t
u
v
w
x
y
z

a **A**

b

c

d

e

f

g

h

i

j

k

l

m

n

o

p

q

r

s

t

u

v

w

x

y

z

antelope antelopes

an animal like a deer, found in Africa

antonym antonyms

a word that means the opposite of another word

anxious

worried

any

one of many; some

apart

away from others; away from each other

ape apes

a large monkey

apologise

apologises, apologising, apologised

to say you are sorry for something you have done or not done

appeal

appeals, appealing, appealed

to ask for something that you are in great need of

appear

appears, appearing, appeared

1 to come into view
2 to seem to be

appetite

the wish to eat

applaud

applauds, applauding, applauded

to clap your hands together to show pleasure

apple apples

a round hard fruit

appoint

appoints, appointing, appointed

to give a job to

appointment

appointments

a time set aside to see someone (for example, a dentist)

approach

approaches, approaching, approached

to come near to

apricot apricots

a round, soft and yellow or orange fruit with a large hard seed called a stone inside it

apron aprons

something you wear over your clothes to keep them clean

aquarium aquariums

a glass or plastic container in which fish are kept

arch arches

1 part of a building or bridge with a curved top and straight sides
2 to bend your body

architect architects

a person who makes the plans for a building

area areas

1 a piece of land or sea
2 the size of a surface

argument arguments

a disagreement; a fight with words

arithmetic

working with numbers; adding, subtracting, multiplying and dividing

arm arms

the part of the body between the shoulder and the hand

armour

a covering of metal worn by soldiers in battle in the old days

arms

weapons

army armies

a large number of soldiers

around

round the edges of; on all sides

arouse

arouses, arousing, aroused

to wake from sleep

arrange

arranges, arranging, arranged

1 to put things in order
2 to make plans to do something

arrest

arrests, arresting, arrested

to make someone a prisoner

arrive

arrives, arriving, arrived

to reach the place you are going to

arrow arrows

1 the straight sharp piece of wood that is shot from a bow
2 a sign shaped like an arrow to show direction

art

the making of pictures or sculptures; art is sometimes a school subject

artery arteries

one of the thin tubes that carry blood away from your heart

article articles

1 a thing
2 a piece of writing in a newspaper or magazine

artificial (say 'artifishul')

not natural; made by people

artist artists

a person who makes pictures or sculptures

ash ashes

1 the grey powder left after a fire
2 a kind of large tree

ashamed

feeling bad about something you have done or not done

ashore

on land

aside

to one side

ask

asks, asking, asked

1 to put a question to
2 **ask for** to say that you want something

asleep

sleeping

a A
b
c
d
e
f
g
h
i
j
k
l
m
n
o
p
q
r
s
t
u
v
w
x
y
z

assembly assemblies

a large group of people who have gathered together

assist

assists, assisting, assisted

to help

assistant assistants

someone who helps

astonish

astonishes, astonishing, astonished

to surprise very much

astray

not in the right place

astronaut astronauts

a person who flies in a spaceship

athletics

sports such as running or jumping

atlas atlases

a book of maps

atmosphere

the air round the earth

attach

attaches, attaching, attached

to fix on to something

attack

attacks, attacking, attacked

to hurt someone or to start a fight

attempt

attempts, attempting, attempted

to try

attend

attends, attending, attended

1 to be present
2 **attend to** to look after

attention

1 care given to doing a job
2 **pay attention** to listen carefully

attic attics

a room just under the roof of a house

attract

attracts, attracting, attracted

1 to win the liking of
2 to make things come closer

audience audiences

people who listen to or watch a performance (a concert or a play, for example)

aunt aunts

a father's or mother's sister; the wife of an uncle

author authors

a person who writes books

authority

the power to make people do what you want

autograph autographs

the special way in which a person handwrites his or her own name. Some people collect autographs.

automatic

working by itself

autumn

the season between summer and winter

available

able to be used or seen

avalanche avalanches

a large amount of snow, ice, rocks or earth suddenly rushing down a mountain

avenue avenues

a road, especially one with trees along the sides

average

usual; ordinary

avoid

avoids, avoiding, avoided

to keep away from

awake

not sleeping

award awards

a prize for something you have done

aware

knowing about something

away

not here; not present

awful

very bad

awkward

1 clumsy
2 difficult to use or deal with

axe axes

a sharp-edged piece of metal on a long handle, used for chopping wood

axle axles

the bar that joins the wheels of a vehicle

bB

baby babies

a very young child

back

1 the part furthest from the front
2 the part of the body between the neck and the bottom of the spine

backbone backbones

the long row of bones down the middle of your back; the spine

backpack backpacks

a bag you can carry on your back; a rucksack

backwards

the opposite way from normal, the wrong way round

bacon

salted or smoked meat from the back or sides of a pig

bad

worse, worst

not good

badge badges

a special sign you wear (to show your school or club, for example)

badger badgers

an animal that has a black and white face and burrows in the ground

a
b B
c
d
e
f
g
h
i
j
k
l
m
n
o
p
q
r
s
t
u
v
w
x
y
z

a
b B
c
d
e
f
g
h
i
j
k
l
m
n
o
p
q
r
s
t
u
v
w
x
y
z

badminton

a game like tennis, played indoors with a shuttlecock

bag bags

a soft container with a top that can be opened

baggage

bags and cases used when travelling

bail

bails, bailing, bailed

1 to empty water from the bottom of a boat
2 money given so that a prisoner can be released until the trial
3 a small piece of wood placed on the stumps in cricket

bait

baits, baiting, baited

to use something in a trap or on a hook to attract an animal or a fish

bake

bakes, baking, baked

to cook in an oven

balance

balances, balancing, balanced

1 to stay steady
2 a piece of equipment that weighs things

balcony balconies

1 a raised area where people sit in a theatre or cinema
2 an outdoor platform reached from an upstairs floor of a building

bald

balder, baldest

having no hair on the head

bale bales

a large amount of goods or material tied together

ball balls

1 a round object, often used in games
2 a special event with dancing

ballet

a graceful dance that may tell a story

balloon balloons

1 a toy of thin rubber that can be blown up
2 a round bag that rises when filled with hot air or gas

ballot ballots

a kind of secret vote to choose someone

bamboo

a kind of grass with stiff hollow stems

ban

bans, banning, banned

not to allow something

banana bananas

a long curved fruit with a yellow skin

band bands

1 a group of people who make music
2 a strip of material used as a decoration or to hold things together
3 a group of people

bandage bandages

a strip of material used to wind round a cut or wound to protect it

bang bangs

1 a sharp blow
2 a sudden loud noise

bangle bangles

a kind of bracelet

banish

banishes, banishing, banished

to send away for a long time as a punishment, especially out of a country

banister banisters

a handrail beside stairs

banjo banjos

a musical instrument like a circular guitar, played by plucking the strings

bank banks

1 the side of a river
2 a place where money is looked after
3 a pile of earth or sand with sloping sides

banner banners

a flag hanging from a pole, mast or rope

banquet banquets

a feast; a large public meal

bar bars

1 a rod of metal or wood
2 a division in music
3 a counter where drinks are served

barbecue (BBQ)
barbecues (BBQs)

a grill used to cook food outdoors

bare

barer, barest

1 having no clothes or covering on
2 empty

bargain bargains

something bought cheaply

barge barges

a boat with a flat bottom, used on a canal or river

bark

1 the noise made by a dog
2 the hard covering round a tree or branch

barley

a kind of grain used as food and for making drinks such as beer

barn barns

a building on a farm used to store crops (for example, grain)

barrel barrels

a large container, shaped like a cylinder

barrier barriers

something that stops you going somewhere (a fence or a gate, for example)

barrow barrows

a small cart that is pushed

base bases

1 the bottom part
2 where someone or something started out from

basement basements

a room or space under a building; a cellar

basin basins

a round and wide container, usually used for washing things in

basket baskets

a bag or container made of woven strips of wood or straw

basketball

a game in which two teams try to throw a ball through a high metal hoop

bat bats

1 the piece of wood used to strike a ball in some games (cricket, for example)
2 a small mouse-like animal that flies at night
3 to hit with a bat

batch batches

a number of things together

bath baths

a water container you can lie or sit in to wash yourself

bathe

bathes, bathing, bathed

1 to swim or play in water
2 to wash

battery batteries

a closed container that stores electricity

battle battles

a fight between two large groups of people

bay bays

a place where the shore curves in

bazaar bazaars

1 a market in Eastern countries
2 a sale of goods to raise money (for a charity or a school, for example)

beach beaches

land by the sea, covered with sand or small stones

bead beads

a small piece of coloured glass, wood or plastic that can be threaded onto a string

beak beaks

the hard pointed mouth of a bird

beam beams

1 a large and heavy piece of wood or metal
2 a ray of light

bean beans

a seed of the bean plant, used for food

bear bears

a large hairy animal with very strong teeth and claws

beard beards

hair growing on a man's chin

beast beasts

an animal

beat

beats, beating, beat

1 to hit again and again
2 to keep time in music
3 to do better than someone in a game or fight

beautiful

very pretty; very pleasant to see or hear

beaver beavers

a furry animal with a wide flat tail that lives in or near water in cool areas

because

used when you give a reason why

bed beds

1 a piece of furniture for sleeping on
2 a part of a garden where plants are grown
3 the bottom of the sea or of a river

bee bees

an insect that makes honey and can sting you

beech

a kind of tree with smooth grey bark

beef

meat from cattle

beer

a strong drink made from barley

beetle beetles

an insect with wings that fold to form a hard cover when it is not flying

beetroot beetroots

a dark red vegetable sometimes used in salads

before

1 in front of; earlier than
2 in past times

beg

begs, begging, begged

to ask someone for money

beggar beggars

someone who lives by begging

begin

begins, beginning, began

to start

behave

behaves, behaving, behaved

to act in a certain way, especially to act well towards others

behaviour

the way you behave

behind

at the back of; on the other side of

being beings

something that is alive

belief beliefs

what you feel sure is true

believe

believes, believing, believed

to feel sure that something is true; to trust in something

bell bells

1 a piece of metal, rounded like a cup, that rings when you swing or hit it
2 an electrical device that is rung to attract attention

belong

belongs, belonging, belonged

1 to be your own
2 to be a part of

a

b B

c

d

e

f

g

h

i

j

k

l

m

n

o

p

q

r

s

t

u

v

w

x

y

z

below

lower down; under

belt belts

a narrow strip of material or leather, worn round the waist

bench benches

1 a long wooden seat
2 a work table

bend bends

1 a turn; a curve in a road
2 to make something curved or crooked

benefit

benefits, benefiting, benefited

to do good to

berry berries

a small juicy fruit

beside

at the side of; next to

besides

also; too

betray

betrays, betraying, betrayed

to give away someone's secret

better

best

1 finer than; nicer than
2 less ill than you were

between

1 in the middle of (two things, people or times, for example)
2 shared by two people

beware

be very careful of

beyond

farther on than

Bible Bibles

the religious book of Christians

bicycle (bike)
bicycles (bikes)

a two-wheeled machine that you sit on to ride

big

bigger, biggest

large in size; the opposite of small

bill bills

1 a piece of paper that shows the money you owe for something
2 the beak of a large bird

bin bins

a large container for putting rubbish in

bind

binds, binding, bound

to wrap round with tape or string

binoculars

a special pair of glasses that helps you to see far into the distance

biology

the science of living things; biology is sometimes a school subject

birch birches

a tree with a silvery-coloured bark

bird birds

an animal with feathers and wings. Most birds can fly.

birth

the time when you start living

birthday birthdays

the day of the year when a person was born

biscuit biscuits

a dry thin cake

bishop bishops

the priest in charge of a large district such as a city

bit bits

a small piece

bite

bites, biting, bit

to cut something with the teeth

bitter

tasting sour; not sweet

black

the darkest colour; the opposite of white

blackberry blackberries

a small juicy fruit that grows on brambles

blackbird blackbirds

a kind of bird. The male has black feathers.

blackboard blackboards

a dark board that you can write on with chalk

blade blades

the part of a knife or sword used for cutting

blame

blames, blaming, blamed

to find fault with; to say who has done wrong

blank

empty; with nothing written or shown on it

blanket blankets

a large warm covering, often made of wool

blast

blasts, blasting, blasted

1 to break something up by explosions
2 a sudden rush of wind
3 a sudden loud noise

blaze

blazes, blazing, blazed

to burn with bright flames

blazer blazers

a kind of jacket, sometimes with a badge on its top pocket

bleach

bleaches, bleaching, bleached

to make something lighter or whiter in colour

bleak

bleaker, bleakest

cold and dismal

bleat bleats

the sound made by sheep and lambs

bleed

bleeds, bleeding, bled

to lose blood

blend

blends, blending, blended

to mix together

a
b B
c
d
e
f
g
h
i
j
k
l
m
n
o
p
q
r
s
t
u
v
w
x
y
z

bless
blesses, blessing, blessed

1 to wish happiness to
2 to ask God to help somebody

blessing blessings

1 something you are glad about
2 asking or receiving God's help

blind blinds

1 not able to see
2 a covering for a window

blindfold blindfolds

a covering for the eyes to stop you seeing

blink
blinks, blinking, blinked

to open and close the eyes quickly

blister blisters

a sore swelling on the skin, with liquid inside it

blizzard blizzards

a strong wind with heavy snow

block blocks

1 a thick piece of something, such as wood or stone
2 to be in the way of
3 one part of a large building or group of buildings

blog blogs

a website where you can read a diary that the writer keeps up to date. Often you can add your own comments.

blond, blonde
blonder, blondest

having light-coloured hair

blood

the red liquid that moves round your body

blossom blossoms

the flowers on plants and trees

blot blots

a dirty mark, especially an ink stain

blow
blows, blowing, blew

1 to shoot air out of the mouth
2 a hit made with the hand or a weapon
3 to move air quickly (for example, the wind blows)

blue

the colour of the sky without clouds

bluebell bluebells

a wild flower; in spring it has small blue flowers shaped like bells

blunder blunders

a stupid mistake

blunt
blunter, bluntest

not able to cut; not sharp

blurb blurbs

information about a book that is written on the back cover

blush
blushes, blushing, blushed

to go red because you are ashamed, excited or shy

board boards

a flat piece of wood

boast

boasts, boasting, boasted

to speak too proudly about yourself or something that belongs to you

boat boats

a small ship

body bodies

1 the whole of a person or animal
2 the main part of the body, ignoring the head, arms, legs

bodyguard bodyguards

a person whose job it is to keep someone safe

bog bogs

wet earth; a swamp

boil

boils, boiling, boiled

1 to cook in hot water
2 to heat water until it starts turning into steam
3 a painful swelling on the body

bold

bolder, boldest

brave; not afraid

bolt bolts

1 a sliding metal bar that keeps a door shut
2 a metal screw
3 to fasten a door
4 to do something suddenly and very fast

bomb bombs

a weapon that is made to explode

bone bones

one of the hard parts of the body that make up the skeleton

bonfire bonfires

a large fire built in the open air

bonnet bonnets

the cover of a car engine

book books

1 a number of pages fastened together
2 to arrange for a seat to be kept for you (at the cinema, for example)

boom booms

a loud hollow noise

boomerang boomerangs

a curved weapon from Australia that can be made to return to the thrower

boot boots

1 a foot covering that comes above the ankle
2 a place for luggage at the back of a car

border borders

the edge of something

bore

bores, boring, bored

1 to make a hole
2 to make someone feel fed up (by talking in a dull way, for example)

born

when something or somebody is first alive

borrow

borrows, borrowing, borrowed

to use something belonging to someone else with their agreement

boss bosses

the person in charge

bossy

bossier, bossiest

ordering other people about

bother

bothers, bothering, bothered

1 to annoy
2 trouble

bottle bottles

a container for liquids, usually with a narrow neck

bottom

1 the lowest part of something
2 the part of your body that you sit on

boulder boulders

a large stone or rock

bounce

bounces, bouncing, bounced

to make something spring up and down

bound

bounds, bounding, bounded

1 to spring upwards and forwards
2 tied together
3 **bound to** very likely to

boundary boundaries

1 the outside edge (of a cricket field, for example)
2 the line where one piece of land touches another

bouquet (say 'bookay')
bouquets

a special bunch of flowers

bow (sounds like 'low') bows

1 a knot with two loops on it
2 a weapon used to fire arrows
3 the special stick used when playing a violin

bow (sounds like 'now') bows

1 the front part of a boat
2 to bend forward from the waist in front of people you think are important

bowl bowls

1 a deep round dish
2 in a ball game (cricket, for example), to send the ball to the person batting
3 the ball used in the game of bowls

bowls

a game in which a large heavy ball is rolled along the grass

box boxes

1 container, usually with a lid; often made of wood, plastic, cardboard or metal
2 to fight with the fists

boy boys

a young male child

bracelet bracelets

a piece of jewellery worn round the wrist or arm

bracket brackets

a support for a shelf

brackets

curved lines like this ( ), which you sometimes put round words or figures

brag

brags, bragging, bragged

to boast a lot

brain brains

the part of the head used for thinking

brake brakes

the part of a vehicle that makes it go slower or stop

bramble brambles

a prickly bush on which blackberries grow

branch branches

the part of a tree on which the leaves grow

brand brands

a particular kind of goods made by one company

brass

a yellowish metal made by mixing copper and zinc

brave

braver, bravest

not afraid; ready to face up to danger or pain

bravery

courage; doing something without fear

bread

a baked food made from flour

break

breaks, breaking, broke

1 to make something fall to pieces or damage something so it stops working
2 a short rest from what you are doing

breakfast

the first meal of the day

breast

the upper front part of the body

breath breaths

air taken in and let out of your lungs

breathe

breathes, breathing, breathed

to take air in and let it out of your lungs

breed

breeds, breeding, bred

1 to have and bring up young ones
2 the family or kind of an animal (a dove is a breed of bird, for example)

breeze breezes

a gentle wind

bribe

bribes, bribing, bribed

to give someone money so that they will help you dishonestly

brick bricks

1 a baked clay block used for building
2 a plastic or wooden block used as a toy

a b B c d e f g h i j k l m n o p q r s t u v w x y z

bride brides

a woman on her wedding day

bridegroom (groom) bridegrooms (grooms)

a man on his wedding day

bridesmaid bridesmaids

a girl or young woman who helps the bride at her wedding

bridge bridges

1 something built to let you cross over a river, road or railway
2 where the captain stands on a ship

bridle bridles

leather band put on a horse's head to control it

brief

briefer, briefest

short

briefs

short underpants

bright

brighter, brightest

1 shining
2 clever

brilliant

1 very bright; shining
2 very clever

brim brims

1 the top edge of a container such as a basin
2 the part of a hat that sticks out at the edge

bring

brings, bringing, brought

to take with you

brisk

brisker, briskest

quick; lively

bristles

short stiff hairs like those on a brush

brittle

easily broken, yet hard

broad

broader, broadest

very wide

broadband

a way of sending and receiving information, sound and video at the same time; a quick way of connecting to the internet

broadcast broadcasts

a radio or television programme

broken

in pieces

bronze

a metal made by mixing copper and tin

brooch (say 'broach') brooches

an ornament that can be pinned to your clothing

brood

broods, brooding, brooded

1 to think deeply and to worry when there is no need to do so
2 a number of young birds hatched together

brook brooks

a small stream

broom brooms

a stiff brush with a long handle

brother brothers

a boy or man who has the same parents as someone else

brow brows

1 the forehead
2 the top of a hill

brown

the colour of earth and of chocolate

bruise bruises

a mark on the skin where it has been hit

brush brushes

1 something you use to tidy your hair
2 a kind of tool used for sweeping, scrubbing and painting
3 a fox's tail

Brussels sprouts

a vegetable like very small cabbages growing on a long stalk

bubble bubbles

1 a hollow ball of liquid filled with air or gas
2 to give off bubbles, like water when it boils

buck bucks

a male deer or rabbit

bucket buckets

a container with a handle, used for carrying liquids

buckle buckles

a metal device that you use to fasten a belt or shoe

bud buds

a leaf or flower before it opens

budgerigar (budgie) budgerigars (budgies)

a small brightly-coloured bird often kept as a pet

bug bugs

1 a small insect
2 an illness
3 an error in a computer

buggy buggies

a pushchair that folds up flat

bugle bugles

a brass musical instrument like a small trumpet

build

builds, building, built

to put up; to make into something

building buildings

something with walls and a roof

bulb bulbs

1 a root that is shaped like an onion
2 the part of an electric light that shines

bulge

bulges, bulging, bulged

to swell outwards

bull bulls

a male cow, elephant or whale

a
b B
c
d
e
f
g
h
i
j
k
l
m
n
o
p
q
r
s
t
u
v
w
x
y
z

b B

a c d e f g h i j k l m n o p q r s t u v w x y z

bulldozer bulldozers

a large vehicle used for moving earth

bullet bullets

a small piece of metal shot from a gun

bully bullies

someone who hurts or frightens other people

bump bumps

1 a sudden knock
2 a swelling on the body where it has been hit

bumper bumpers

a part at the front and back of a vehicle that protects it from knocks

bun buns

a small round bread roll or cake

bunch bunches

several things tied together

bundle bundles

many things tied or held together

bungalow bungalows

a house with no upstairs floors

bunk bed bunk beds

two beds, one fixed above the other

burden burdens

something heavy that is carried; a load

burger burgers

a flattened portion of minced meat, grilled and served in a bun

burglar burglars

a person who enters houses and shops to steal

burial burials

the burying of a dead body

burn

burns, burning, burnt, burned

1 to be on fire or to set on fire
2 a place where something very hot has damaged your skin

burrow burrows

a tunnel dug under the ground by an animal (a rabbit, for example)

burst

bursts, bursting, burst

1 to blow into pieces
2 to break something open on purpose

bury

buries, burying, buried

to put something in a hole in the ground and cover it over

bus buses

a large vehicle that carries lots of passengers

bush bushes

a small tree

bushy

very thick

business businesses

work; trade

busy
busier, busiest

having no time to spare; doing a lot of things

butcher butchers

a person who sells meat

butter

a fatty food made from cream; you can put it on bread

buttercup buttercups

a bright-yellow wild flower

butterfly butterflies

an insect with four large wings, which are sometimes brightly coloured

button buttons

a small round object that is used to do up clothing

buy
buys, buying, bought

to get something by giving money

buzz

a low sound that is like the sound made by some insects when flying (for example, bees)

buzzer buzzers

an electrical device that makes a buzzing sound

bypass bypasses

a road that takes traffic round a town or village instead of going through it

cC

cab cabs

1 a place for the driver of a lorry or train
2 a taxi

cabbage cabbages

a large vegetable with broad leaves that together make a ball shape

cabin cabins

1 a room on a boat or an aeroplane
2 a small wooden house

cable cables

1 special wires that carry electricity, telephone calls, television programmes and other electronic information
2 a strong rope often made of wires twisted together

cackle
cackles, cackling, cackled

to laugh or make some other noise sounding like a hen after it lays an egg

cactus cacti

a prickly desert plant with a thick stem

cadet cadets

a young person being trained in the police, army or navy

café cafés

a place for eating simple meals or snacks

cage cages

a box or room made of wires or bars in which animals or birds are kept

cake cakes

a sweet food made of fat, flour, eggs and sugar and baked in an oven

calculator calculators

a small electronic machine used for solving number problems

calendar calendars

a printed sheet or book listing the days and months of the year

calf calves

1 a young animal, usually a young cow or bull
2 the soft back part of the leg between the knee and the ankle

call

calls, calling, called

1 to shout to
2 to visit
3 to give a name to

calm

calmer, calmest

quiet and still; peaceful

camel camels

a large animal with a hump, used for carrying people and goods in the desert

camera cameras

a piece of equipment for taking photographs

camouflage

(say 'camooflaage')

a form of dress or covering that makes people or things look like part of the surroundings

camp

camps, camping, camped

1 to live in a tent
2 a group of tents together

can cans

a sealed metal container, sometimes used to store food or drink

canal canals

a long narrow ditch filled with water for boats to use

canary canaries

a yellow bird that sings

candle candles

a stick of wax with a wick, which is burned to give light

cane canes

the hollow stalk of some plants, sometimes used as a stick

canoe canoes

a light boat moved by using a paddle

canteen canteens

a place where people eat together (for example, in a factory or school)

canvas

strong cloth used to make tents and sails

cap caps
1 a soft hat with a flat brim at the front only
2 a lid or cover

capable
able to do

capacity
how much something holds

capital capitals
1 the chief city or town
2 a large letter (such as A)

captain captains
1 the person who controls a plane or a ship
2 an officer in the army
3 the leader of a team or group

caption captions
words put next to a picture

capture
captures, capturing, captured
to catch and then keep

car cars
a vehicle that will carry about five people

caramel
a chewy sweet or toffee

caravan caravans
a small house on wheels, which can be pulled by a vehicle

card cards
1 a piece of stiff thick paper
2 a piece of card with a message and often a picture
3 one of a set of cards used for playing games

cardboard
strong thick paper often used for making things

cardigan cardigans
a knitted woollen jacket that keeps you warm

care
cares, caring, cared
1 to be concerned about someone or something
2 the act of looking after someone or something

careful
doing something with care; thinking about what you are doing and trying to do it well

careless
doing something without care; not thinking about what you are doing

carer carers
a person who looks after another person (a child, for example)

caretaker caretakers
a person who looks after a building (a school, for example)

cargo cargos
things carried on a ship or aeroplane

carnation carnations
a sweet-smelling garden flower, usually pink, white or red

carnival carnivals
a large procession, usually in fancy dress

a
b
c C
d
e
f
g
h
i
j
k
l
m
n
o
p
q
r
s
t
u
v
w
x
y
z

carol carols

a Christmas song

carpenter carpenters

someone who makes things out of wood

carpet carpets

a thick soft covering for a floor

carriage carriages

1 the part of a train where people sit
2 a vehicle pulled by horses

carrot carrots

a long orange root vegetable

carry

carries, carrying, carried

to take from one place to another

cart carts

a vehicle for carrying things, sometimes pulled by a horse

carton cartons

a box made of cardboard

cartoon cartoons

1 a funny drawing in a magazine, book or newspaper
2 a film made out of drawings

carve

carves, carving, carved

1 to shape wood or stone with cutting tools
2 to cut meat into slices

case cases

1 a kind of box used to keep or carry things in
2 a suitcase

cash

money in notes or coins

cast casts

1 the actors in a play or film
2 to throw
3 a mould or hard cover

castle castles

a large building with strong stone walls, built to keep out enemies

cat cats

a small furry animal often kept as a pet

catalogue catalogues

1 a list of things in a special order
2 a book used for shopping by post

catch

catches, catching, caught

1 to take hold of
2 to get an illness

caterpillar caterpillars

a creature that looks like a coloured worm with legs, and will turn into a moth or butterfly

cathedral cathedrals

a very important church

catkin catkins

a kind of fluffy flower that grows on some trees (the willow, for example)

cattle

a group of cows

cauliflower cauliflowers

a vegetable with a large white flower that you can eat

cause

causes, causing, caused

to make something happen

cautious

taking great care

cave caves

a hollow place in rocks or under the ground

CD

see **compact disk**

cease

ceases, ceasing, ceased

to stop doing something

ceiling ceilings

the top part of a room; the roof of a room

celebrate

celebrates, celebrating, celebrated

to remember something in a special way, especially by having a party or feast

celery

a vegetable with long whitish-green stalks

cell cells

a room in which prisoners are kept

cellar cellars

a room under a building, used for storing things

cello (say 'chello') cellos

a wooden musical instrument that looks like a large violin

cell phone cell phones

a phone that you can use anywhere; a mobile phone

Celsius

a temperature scale of 100 degrees, once called centigrade

cement

a stone dust that sets hard when mixed with water

cemetery cemeteries

a place where people are buried

centigrade

a temperature scale of 100 degrees, now called Celsius

centimetre centimetres

a measure of length; 100 centimetres are equal to one metre

centipede centipedes

a crawling creature with a large number of legs

central

1 in the middle
2 important

central heating

a way of warming a building by sending heat through pipes from a central point

centre centres

1 the middle of something
2 a place where people come together to do things

century centuries

1 100 years
2 100 runs in cricket

a b c C d e f g h i j k l m n o p q r s t u v w x y z

cereal cereals
1 a kind of food made from grain and usually eaten for breakfast
2 a crop that is used for food (for example, wheat or rice)

ceremony ceremonies
a formal event held to celebrate something or reward someone

certain
1 sure
2 some, but not all

certificate certificates
a piece of paper that says something important has happened (for example, a birth)

chaffinch chaffinches
a kind of small bird

chain chains
a number of rings joined together

chair chairs
a piece of furniture for one person to sit on

chalk
1 a soft white rock that crumbles
2 a white or coloured stick used for writing on a blackboard

challenge
challenges, challenging, challenged
to test someone's ability

champion champions
the winner of a competition

chance chances
1 an unexpected happening
2 a time when you can do something you want to do

change
changes, changing, changed
1 to start being different
2 money you get back when you pay more than is needed

channel channels
a narrow strip of water

chapatti chapattis
a thin pancake made of bread (an Asian food)

chapter chapters
a part of a story or book

character characters
1 what someone is like as a person
2 a person in a play or story

charge
charges, charging, charged
1 the price asked for something
2 to rush at
3 in charge of in control of something

chariot chariots
a cart pulled by horses, used in battle long ago

charity
giving money or help to people who need it

charm charms
1 a magic spell
2 a small ornament that is supposed to bring good luck

charming
pleasing to other people

chart charts

1 a map used by sailors when they are at sea
2 a piece of paper with information, often a drawing or a diagram

chase

chases, chasing, chased

to run after

chat

chats, chatting, chatted

to talk in a friendly way

chatter

chatters, chattering, chattered

to speak quickly, especially about things that do not matter much

chauffeur chauffeurs

a person whose job it is to drive a car for someone

cheap

cheaper, cheapest

low in price; not costing a lot

cheat

cheats, cheating, cheated

to act unfairly, break the rules or make others believe what is not true

check

checks, checking, checked

1 to make sure that everything is correct and in order
2 a pattern of squares

checkout checkouts

where you pay for shopping in a supermarket

cheek cheeks

1 one of the sides of the face between the nose and the ears
2 rudeness

cheer

cheers, cheering, cheered

to shout loudly for joy

cheerful

full of fun; looking happy

cheese cheeses

a solid food made from milk

chef chefs

the cook in a restaurant

chemist chemists

someone who sells medicines

chemistry

the science of substances; chemistry is sometimes a school subject

cherry cherries

a small red or black fruit with a hard seed called a stone

chess

a board game played by two people on a squared board

chest chests

1 a large strong box
2 the upper front part of the body

chestnut chestnuts

the hard brown seed of the chestnut tree

chew

chews, chewing, chewed

to keep biting food in your mouth

a
b
c C
d
e
f
g
h
i
j
k
l
m
n
o
p
q
r
s
t
u
v
w
x
y
z

chick chicks

a young bird

chicken chickens

a young hen kept for its eggs and meat

chickenpox

an illness that gives you itchy spots and a high temperature

chief chiefs

1 the person in charge
2 the most important

child children

a young boy or girl

chill

1 coldness
2 a slight cold that makes you shiver

chilli chillies

a small hot-tasting seed pod, sometimes used in sauces

chilly
chillier, chilliest

rather cold (weather, for example)

chime chimes

the noise made by bells

chimney chimneys

a tall pipe that takes smoke away from a fire

chimpanzee chimpanzees

a kind of monkey without a tail

chin chins

the part of the face below the bottom lip

china

fine pottery, especially cups, saucers and plates

chip chips

1 a long piece of potato fried in deep fat
2 a tiny piece broken from something larger

chirp

a noise made by young birds and some insects (for example, grasshoppers)

chisel chisels

a sharp steel tool used for cutting wood, stone or metal

chocolate

a sweet food or drink made from cocoa seeds

choice choices

the act of choosing; something you choose

choir choirs

a group of people singing together

choke
chokes, choking, choked

1 to be unable to breathe because of something in your throat
2 to block up

choose
chooses, choosing, chose

to pick out what you want from two or more things

chop
chops, chopping, chopped

1 to cut with an axe or knife
2 a slice of meat with a bone in it

chopsticks

two small sticks used for eating food (Chinese food, for example)

chorus choruses

1 part of a song or poem that is repeated after each verse
2 a group of people singing together

christening

when a baby is given its name in a Christian church

Christian Christians

a believer in Jesus Christ

Christmas

Christian festival in December

chuckle

chuckles, chuckling, chuckled

to laugh quietly

chunk chunks

a thick piece cut off from something larger

church churches

a building in which Christians worship God

cider

a strong drink made from apples

cinder cinders

a piece of coal that has been partly burned

cinema cinemas

a place where films are shown

circle circles

a round flat shape

circumference

circumferences

the outside edge of a circle

circus circuses

a travelling show of acrobats, clowns and sometimes animals

citizenship

the things that people are allowed to do and the things that they are expected to do; citizenship is sometimes a school subject

city cities

a large town

claim

claims, claiming, claimed

to ask for something that belongs to you

clang

clangs, clanging, clanged

the sound made by a large bell

clap

claps, clapping, clapped

1 to slap the hands together quickly
2 the sound made by thunder

clarinet clarinets

a musical instrument played by blowing

clash

clashes, clashing, clashed

to bump together noisily

clasp

clasps, clasping, clasped

1 to grip or hold tightly
2 a fastening

a b c C d e f g h i j k l m n o p q r s t u v w x y z

a
b
c C
d
e
f
g
h
i
j
k
l
m
n
o
p
q
r
s
t
u
v
w
x
y
z

class classes

people who are taught together

classroom classrooms

the room at school where your lessons take place

clatter

a loud rattling noise

claw claws

the sharp hard nail of a bird or an animal

clay

sticky earth from which bricks and pottery may be made

clean

cleaner, cleanest

not dirty or dusty

cleaner cleaners

a man or woman who cleans the inside of a building

clear

clearer, clearest

1 easy to see, hear or understand
2 to put away; to tidy

clergy

church ministers

clerk (say 'clark') clerks

a person who attends to letters and papers in an office

clever

cleverer, cleverest

1 quick at learning and understanding things
2 skilful

click clicks

1 a small sharp noise
2 to press and release a button on the mouse when you are using a computer

cliff cliffs

high steep land, often overlooking the sea

climate climates

the sort of weather a place usually has

climb

climbs, climbing, climbed

to go up a steep place (a mountain or a hill, for example)

cling

clings, clinging, clung

to hold on tightly

clinic clinics

a place where doctors and nurses give help to people

clip

clips, clipping, clipped

1 to cut with a pair of shears or scissors
2 something that fastens things together

cloak cloaks

a loose covering without sleeves for the body and arms

clock clocks

a machine that shows the time

clockwork

machinery that is worked by winding a spring

close (sounds like 'd**ose**')

closer, closest

near

close (sounds like 'd**oze**')

closes, closing, closed

to shut

cloth cloths

1 material (for making clothes or curtains, for example)
2 a piece of cloth used for cleaning

clothes

things that you wear on your body (for example, trousers)

cloud clouds

a mass of rainy mist or smoke that is floating in the sky

clover

a small flowering plant

clown clowns

a person who acts foolishly to make people laugh

club clubs

1 a heavy stick
2 a group of people who meet together for a special reason
3 a stick used to play golf
4 one of the four kinds in a pack of playing cards

clue clues

something that helps you to find the answer to a puzzle or a question

clumsy

clumsier, clumsiest

awkward in the way you move or do things

cluster clusters

a bunch or a group of things

coach coaches

1 a passenger vehicle that is like a bus
2 a person who gives special training (to a football team, for example)

coal

a black rock dug out of the ground and burned to make heat

coarse

coarser, coarsest

rough; not fine

coast coasts

the strip of land next to the sea

coat coats

1 a piece of clothing with sleeves, worn over other clothes
2 the hair of an animal

cobweb cobwebs

a net made by a spider to trap insects

cock cocks

a male bird

cocoa

1 a powder made from the seed of a cocoa tree
2 hot chocolate; a drink made from cocoa and milk or water

coconut coconuts

a hard and hairy fruit that is white inside; it grows on a special kind of palm tree

a
b
c C
d
e
f
g
h
i
j
k
l
m
n
o
p
q
r
s
t
u
v
w
x
y
z

a
b
c C
d
e
f
g
h
i
j
k
l
m
n
o
p
q
r
s
t
u
v
w
x
y
z

cod cod

a large sea fish used as food

code codes

1 writing with a hidden meaning
2 a set of rules

coffee

a drink made from the roasted and crushed seeds of the coffee tree

coffin coffins

a box in which a dead body is put

coil

coils, coiling, coiled

to gather rope, wire or thin pipes in rings, one on top of the other

coin coins

a piece of metal used as money

cold

colder, coldest

1 not hot
2 an illness that makes your nose run

collar collars

1 a leather or metal band put round the neck of an animal
2 the part of your clothes that fits round the neck

collect

collects, collecting, collected

to gather together

collection collections

a number of things gathered in a set

college colleges

a place where students are taught

collide

collides, colliding, collided

to come together with great force

colonel (say 'kernel') colonels

a senior officer in the army

colour colours

one way of saying how things look when seen in daylight (green or red, for example)

column columns

1 a post, usually of stone or wood, used to support a part of a building
2 a vertical strip of printing in a book or newspaper
3 a line of soldiers

comb combs

a thin piece of metal or plastic with many teeth, used to keep hair tidy

combine

combines, combining, combined

to join or mix together

comedian comedians

a person who tells funny stories in public to make people laugh

comedy comedies

a play or film that makes you laugh

comfort

comforts, comforting, comforted

1 to show kindness to someone in pain or trouble
2 a pleasant easy feeling

comfortable

giving or having comfort

comic comics

1 a magazine or paper for young people, with stories told in pictures
2 making you laugh; funny
3 another name for a comedian

comma commas

a punctuation mark shaped like this ,

command

commands, commanding, commanded

to order

commercial

1 to do with buying and selling
2 an advertisement on television or radio or at the cinema

common

commoner, commonest

ordinary; usual; found in many places

compact disk (CD)

compact disks (CDs)

a disk containing information, sounds or pictures

companion companions

someone who is with you, often a friend

company companies

1 the people you are with
2 a group of people doing business

compare

compares, comparing, compared

to see if things are alike

compartment compartments

a separate section (in a fridge, for example)

compass compasses

an instrument that tells you where north is

compel

compels, compelling, compelled

to force

competition competitions

a way of finding out who is the best or luckiest at something

complain

complains, complaining, complained

to grumble or say you are unhappy about something

complete

completes, completing, completed

1 to finish altogether
2 the whole with nothing missing

complicated

having a lot of parts; difficult to understand; not simple

compliment compliments

something nice someone says to praise you

composer composers

a person who makes up music

computer computers

a machine that stores information and can work things out quickly

a
b
c C
d
e
f
g
h
i
j
k
l
m
n
o
p
q
r
s
t
u
v
w
x
y
z

conceal
conceals, concealing, concealed
to hide from view

conceited
thinking too much of yourself; too proud

concentrate
concentrates, concentrating, concentrated
to think hard about something

concern
concerns, concerning, concerned
1 to be connected with
2 something you are worried about

concert concerts
music played in front of an audience

concise
brief; short; in a few words

conclusion conclusions
the finish; the end

condition conditions
the state of something or someone

conduct (say 'conduct')
behaviour

conduct (say 'conduct')
conducts, conducting, conducted
to guide; to lead

conductor conductors
a person who is in charge of an orchestra or choir

cone cones
1 the fruit of the fir tree
2 a container for ice cream, wide at the top and pointed at the bottom
3 a solid shape that is round at the bottom and pointed at the top

confess
confesses, confessing, confessed
to talk about something you have done (often something wrong)

confident
feeling sure or safe

confused
not in a clear state of mind; mixed up

congratulate
congratulates, congratulating, congratulated
to tell someone that you are pleased about something good that has happened to him or her

conjuror conjurors
a magician; someone who can do tricks

conker conkers
a brown nut; the seed of a horse chestnut tree

connect
connects, connecting, connected
to join together

connective connectives
a word that links one phrase, sentence or paragraph to another

conquer
conquers, conquering, conquered
to defeat others

conscience

the feeling inside you that tells you if something is right or wrong

conscious

awake; knowing what is happening

consent

consents, consenting, consented

to agree to something

consider

considers, considering, considered

to think carefully

consonant consonants

a letter that is not a, e, i, o or u

construct

constructs, constructing, constructed

to build

contact lens contact lenses

a small plastic disc worn in the eye to help you see better

contain

contains, containing, contained

to have inside; to hold

container containers

a box or jar that you can put things in

content (say 'content')

quite pleased; satisfied with things as they are

contents (say 'contents')

what something contains

contest contests

a competition to find the best or the winner

continent continents

one of the large land masses of the world (Europe, Asia or Africa, for example)

continue

continues, continuing, continued

to go on with; to go on; to last

control

controls, controlling, controlled

to guide; to keep steady

convenient

suitable

convent convents

the building in which nuns live

conversation conversations

talk between two or more people

convict (say 'convict') convicts

a criminal in prison

convict (say 'convict')

convicts, convicting, convicted

to find someone guilty of a crime

convince

convinces, convincing, convinced

to make someone believe something

cook

cooks, cooking, cooked

1 to make food ready to eat by heating it
2 a person who cooks

cool

cooler, coolest

not quite cold

a b **c C** d e f g h i j k l m n o p q r s t u v w x y z

a
b
c C
d
e
f
g
h
i
j
k
l
m
n
o
p
q
r
s
t
u
v
w
x
y
z

copper
1 a soft, reddish-brown metal
2 the colour of this metal

copy
copies, copying, copied
1 to do the same as somebody else; to imitate
2 to make something the same as something else

cord cords
a piece of thick string or thin rope

core cores
the part in the centre of something

cork
1 the light thick bark of the cork tree
2 a piece of this used to close the mouth of a bottle

corn
1 the seeds of grain, which are used as food
2 a sore hard place on the foot

corner corners
where two roads, lines or walls meet

corpse corpses
a dead body

correct
1 quite right, true
2 to make something right

corridor corridors
a narrow covered passage that joins rooms together

cost
how much you must pay to buy something

costume costumes
clothes worn for a special reason

cosy
cosier, cosiest
comfortable and warm

cot cots
a baby's bed with high sides

cottage cottages
a small house, often in the country

cotton
1 a kind of light cloth made from a plant grown in warm countries
2 thread used for sewing

couch couches
a soft seat made for more than one person; a sofa; a settee

cough
coughs, coughing, coughed
to force air from the chest and lungs with a noise

council councils
a group of people chosen to plan and decide what should be done (in a town or district, for example)

count
counts, counting, counted
to number in the proper order; to add up

counter counters
1 a table over which things are served in a shop
2 a small disc used in counting and in games

country countries

1 the part of a land that is away from towns
2 the whole of a land (for example, Poland or China)

county counties

a part of England, Wales or Ireland

couple couples

two of something

coupon coupons

a ticket that can be exchanged for something of value

courage

bravery

course courses

1 one part of a meal (for example, dessert)
2 a large area of land where certain sports take place (for example, golf, horse racing)
3 the direction something takes

court courts

1 a piece of ground on which certain games are played (for example, a tennis court)
2 a place where trials are held
3 the place where a king and queen live; the people who help the king and queen

cousin cousins

the child of an uncle or aunt

cover

covers, covering, covered

to put something over something else

cow cows

1 a large female animal kept on farms for its milk and meat
2 the female of some other animals (for example, the elephant or the whale)

coward cowards

a person who runs away from danger or difficulty

crab crabs

a kind of shellfish with ten legs

crack cracks

1 a thin break
2 a sharp noise like something hard breaking

cracker crackers

1 a thin biscuit
2 a special tube covered in paper, popular at parties. When pulled apart it makes a bang and small gifts fall out.

cradle cradles

a rocking bed for a baby

craft crafts

a job or trade needing skill, especially with the hands; craft is sometimes a school subject

crafty

craftier, craftiest

not to be trusted; cunning

cranberry cranberries

a tiny red berry with lots of juice

crane cranes

1 a tall machine for lifting heavy things
2 a large water bird with long legs

a
b
c C
d
e
f
g
h
i
j
k
l
m
n
o
p
q
r
s
t
u
v
w
x
y
z

crash

crashes, crashing, crashed

1 to hit against and be smashed
2 a loud noise made by something breaking

crawl

crawls, crawling, crawled

1 to move on the hands and knees
2 to move slowly
3 a special way of swimming

crayon crayons

a coloured pencil or a stick of coloured wax for drawing with

crazy

crazier, craziest

1 mad; without sense
2 likely to do strange or silly things

cream

1 a liquid like milk but thicker
2 the colour of cream

crease creases

1 the mark made by folding cloth
2 a mark on a cricket pitch

create

creates, creating, created

to make something new

creature creatures

an animal of any kind (including birds, insects and fish)

creep

creeps, creeping, crept

1 to move along close to the ground
2 to move carefully, usually to avoid being seen or heard

crescent crescents

1 part of the edge of a circle; the shape of the new moon
2 a curved street

crest crests

1 the top of something, especially the top of a wave or a hill
2 feathers on the top of something

crew crews

a team of people who do the work on a ship or a plane

cricket

1 an outdoor game played with a ball and a bat
2 a jumping insect that chirps

crime crimes

the breaking of the law

criminal criminals

a person who breaks the law

crimson

a deep red colour

crisis crises (say 'crisees')

a time when something serious or dangerous happens

crisp crisps

1 a very thin slice of potato cooked in oil and eaten as a snack
2 firm and dry

crockery

dishes, especially plates, cups and saucers

crocodile crocodiles

a large and dangerous animal with a scaly skin. It is found in some hot countries, especially in rivers.

crocus crocuses

a small spring flower that is yellow, purple or white

crook crooks

1 a person who commits a crime; a criminal
2 a shepherd's stick with a hook at one end

crooked

1 bent; not straight
2 dishonest

crop crops

1 plants grown for food
2 the amount of these plants gathered at one time
3 to cut something short (for example, hair)

cross

crosses, crossing, crossed

1 to move from one side to the other
2 anything shaped like a x or +
3 angry

crossing

see *zebra crossing*

crouch

crouches, crouching, crouched

to bend down low with your legs bent

crow crows

a large black bird that has a loud rough cry

crowd crowds

a large number of people all together in one place

crown crowns

the special head-dress of a king or queen, often made of gold

cruel

crueller, cruellest

very unkind

cruise cruises

a long journey by boat

crumb crumbs

a tiny piece of bread or cake

crumble

crumbles, crumbling, crumbled

to break into little pieces

crush

crushes, crushing, crushed

to press together very tightly; to squash

crust crusts

the hard outside part of anything, especially of bread

crutch crutches

a wood or metal support used by some people to help them walk

cry

cries, crying, cried

1 to have tears coming from your eyes; to weep
2 to call out
3 a noise made by a person or animal

cub cubs

a young animal such as a fox, wolf or lion

cube cubes

a solid square shape

a b **c C** d e f g h i j k l m n o p q r s t u v w x y z

cuckoo cuckoos

a bird that lays its eggs in other birds' nests and makes a sound like its name

cucumber cucumbers

a long green vegetable eaten raw

cuddle

cuddles, cuddling, cuddled

to take into the arms and hug

culprit culprits

a person who is guilty of doing wrong; the person to blame

cunning

clever in a sly way

cupboard cupboards

a set of shelves with doors at the front

cure

cures, curing, cured

to make better somebody who has been ill

curious

1 strange; unusual
2 wanting to know

curl curls

hair that falls into curves

currant currants

1 a small dried grape often used in puddings and cakes
2 a small red, black or white berry grown on a bush

current currents

a flow of water, air, or electricity

curry curries

a hot-tasting Asian food made of meat and/or vegetables

cursor cursors

a symbol on the computer screen that you can move using the mouse or the keyboard

curtain curtains

a cloth that hangs in front of something (a window, for example)

curve curves

a smooth rounded shape or a bend

cushion cushions

a pillow that may be used on a sofa or chair

custard

a sweet yellow sauce that is eaten with puddings

customer customers

a person who pays money for something (in a shop, for example)

cut

cuts, cutting, cut

to open or divide with something sharp

cute

cuter, cutest

very pretty or sweet

cycle cycles

1 a bicycle
2 to make a bicycle move

cylinder cylinders

a long round shape, like a can

dD

dab

dabs, dabbing, dabbed

to touch lightly

Daddy (Dad)

daddies (dads)

a name for your father

daffodil daffodils

a yellow spring flower grown from a bulb

daily

each day

dairy dairies

1 a place where butter and cheese are made from milk and cream
2 a place where milk is put into bottles

daisy daisies

a small flower with a yellow centre and white petals

dam dams

a wall built to hold back water

damage

damages, damaging, damaged

to harm

damp

damper, dampest

slightly wet

damson damsons

a small dark-purple plum

dance

dances, dancing, danced

to move the body to music; dance is sometimes a school subject

dandelion dandelions

a yellow wild flower

danger dangers

harm; something that can hurt you

dangerous

likely to hurt, harm or kill

dangle

dangles, dangling, dangled

to hang down from something; to swing loosely from something

dare

dares, daring, dared

1 to be brave enough to do something dangerous
2 to ask someone to do something dangerous

dark

darker, darkest

not light or bright

darling darlings

a name for someone you love very much

dart

darts, darting, darted

1 to move very quickly
2 a small arrow thrown at a board in a game

dash

dashes, dashing, dashed

1 to rush from place to place
2 a short line like this – used in writing

date dates

1 the day, month and year when something takes place
2 a sweet brown fruit

daughter daughters

a female child of a parent

dawdle

dawdles, dawdling, dawdled

to do something so slowly that time is wasted

dawn dawns

the very first light of the day; early in the morning

day days

1 a period of 24 hours
2 the time between sunrise and sunset

daybreak

dawn; sunrise

dazed

not knowing where you are (for example, after a blow on the head)

dazzle

dazzles, dazzling, dazzled

to blind for a moment with bright light

dead

no longer alive

deadly

able to cause death

deaf

deafer, deafest

not able to hear

deal

deals, dealing, dealt (say 'delt')

1 to do business with
2 to give out cards in a card game
3 **a great deal** a lot
4 **deal with** to do what has to be done about something

dear

dearer, dearest

1 much loved by someone
2 costing a lot of money

death

the time when you stop living

debt debts

what you owe to someone

decade decades

ten years

deceive

deceives, deceiving, deceived

to fool someone by telling them lies

decent

proper; respectable

decide

decides, deciding, decided

to make up your mind about something

decimals

a way of counting in tens

decision decisions

what you have decided

deck decks

the floor of a boat, a plane or a bus

declare

declares, declaring, declared

to state firmly; to say what you think or what you plan to do

decorate

decorates, decorating, decorated

1 to paint or put wallpaper on the inside of a house
2 to make something look prettier

decoration decorations

something special that you add to make a thing look prettier

decrease

decreases, decreasing, decreased

to make smaller

deed deeds

an action; something done

deep

deeper, deepest

far down, often in water; far inside

deer deer

a large wild animal that can run fast

defeat

defeats, defeating, defeated

to beat in battle or in a game

defend

defends, defending, defended

to protect; to guard

definite

sure; certain

definition definitions

the meaning of a word or phrase

defy

defies, defying, defied

to refuse openly to do what you are told; to refuse to obey an order

degree degrees

a measurement of heat or of an angle

delay

delays, delaying, delayed

1 to put off doing something for a while
2 to make late

delete

deletes, deleting, deleted

to cross out or remove something completely (for example, on a computer)

deliberate

done on purpose

delicate

very fine; easily broken

delicious

having a very pleasant taste or smell

delight

great pleasure; joy

deliver

delivers, delivering, delivered

to bring; to hand over

demand

demands, demanding, demanded

to ask very firmly for something

a b c **d D** e f g h i j k l m n o p q r s t u v w x y z

demonstrate

demonstrates, demonstrating, demonstrated

to show clearly to other people how something should be done

den dens

the place where a wild animal eats and sleeps

denim

strong cotton cloth, usually blue

dense

denser, densest

very thick; too thick to see through

dent dents

a hollow caused by a blow or knock

dentist dentists

a person who looks after teeth

deny

denies, denying, denied

to say firmly that something is not true

departure departures

the moment of leaving or going away

depend

depends, depending, depended

to trust in somebody or something for help

depress

depresses, depressing, depressed

to make someone feel sad

depth

how deep something is

descend

descends, descending, descended

to go down; to come down

describe

describes, describing, described

to say how something or someone looks

description descriptions

words saying what something is

desert (say '**des**ert') deserts

a dry empty place where hardly anything grows because of the heat and lack of water

desert (say 'des**ert**')

deserts, deserting, deserted

to leave when you are expected to stay

deserve

deserves, deserving, deserved

to have earned a reward or punishment by what you have done

design designs

1 a plan or drawing
2 a pattern

desire

desires, desiring, desired

to want something very much

desk desks

a kind of table used for writing at

despair

despairs, despairing, despaired

to lose hope; to give up hope

desperate

ready to do almost anything to get what you want

dessert (say 'de**sert**') desserts

the sweet dish eaten at the end of a meal

destination destinations

the place you are going to; the place that something has been sent to

destroy

destroys, destroying, destroyed

to break up completely

destruction

the act of destroying

detail details

a very small part or fact

detective detectives

a person, usually a police officer, whose job it is to find out who carried out a crime

detergent

a kind of soap for washing clothes or dishes

detest

detests, detesting, detested

to dislike greatly; to hate

develop

develops, developing, developed

to grow; to change gradually

device devices

an object that helps you to do something

dew

drops of water found on the ground and on plants in the early morning

diagram diagrams

a drawing to show how something works or is made

dial dials

1 the face of an object such as a clock or watch, with numbers or letters on it
2 to press the numbers when you make a phone call

dialect dialects

how people speak in a certain district

diamond diamonds

1 a very hard and sparkly jewel, often used in rings
2 a shape with four sloping sides that are the same length
3 one of the four kinds in a pack of playing cards

diary diaries

a book in which you write what happens each day

dice (or **die**) dice

a small square block with dots on each side, used in many games

dictate

dictates, dictating, dictated

1 to tell others what to do
2 to say something for someone else to write down

dictionary dictionaries

a book like this one, with a list of words and their meanings arranged in alphabetical order

die

dies, dying, died

to stop living

a
b
c
d D
e
f
g
h
i
j
k
l
m
n
o
p
q
r
s
t
u
v
w
x
y
z

diet diets

1 the sort of food we eat
2 an eating plan to help you lose weight or be healthier

difference differences

what makes something different

different

not like something else; not the same

difficult

not easy to do or to understand

dig

digs, digging, dug

to turn soil over with a spade

digest

digests, digesting, digested

to break down food in your stomach after you have eaten it

digit digits

the symbol used for writing a number (for example, 1, 2, 3)

dim

dimmer, dimmest

not bright; not easy to see

din

a loud noise of many things together

dinghy dinghies

a small rowing-boat

dinner dinners

the main meal of the day

dinosaur dinosaurs

a large creature that lived millions of years ago

dip

dips, dipping, dipped

1 to place into a liquid for a short time
2 to slope downwards

direct

directs, directing, directed

1 to tell somebody which way to go
2 straight to; short and quick

direction directions

the way you go to get to a place

dirt

mud; dust; something not clean

dirty

dirtier, dirtiest

not clean

disabled

not able to use part of your body or mind properly

disagree

disagrees, disagreeing, disagreed

not to agree with

disappear

disappears, disappearing, disappeared

to go out of sight; to vanish

disappoint

disappoints, disappointing, disappointed

to make somebody sorry because they have not got what they hoped for

disaster disasters

a terrible event, happening or accident

disc (sometimes spelt 'disk')
discs

a round flat object (also see **disk** and **compact disk**)

disco discos

a place where people dance to music

discover

discovers, discovering, discovered

to find out about something; to find for the first time

discuss

discusses, discussing, discussed

to talk about something with other people

disease diseases

an illness

disgraceful

so bad you should be ashamed of it

disguise

disguises, disguising, disguised

to change how you look by altering your face and clothes

disgust

disgusts, disgusting, disgusted

to make somebody feel strongly against something

dish dishes

1 a bowl or plate
2 food served at a meal

dishonest

not honest or trustworthy

dishwasher dishwashers

a machine that washes dishes

disk (sometimes spelt 'disc')
disks

a round flat object, especially the kind that can be used to store information

dislike

dislikes, disliking, disliked

not to like

dismal

dull or sad; not bright

dismiss

dismisses, dismissing, dismissed

to send someone away

display displays

a show; objects set out specially for people to look at

dissolve

dissolves, dissolving, dissolved

to mix completely with a liquid

distance distances

1 somewhere far away
2 the space between two points or places

distinct

1 quite clearly seen or heard
2 different

distress

great trouble, sorrow or unhappiness

district districts

a part of a country or a town

disturb

disturbs, disturbing, disturbed

1 to upset; to worry
2 to put out of order; to interrupt

a
b
c
d D
e
f
g
h
i
j
k
l
m
n
o
p
q
r
s
t
u
v
w
x
y
z

disturbance disturbances

trouble; an upset

ditch ditches

a long narrow hole in the ground

dive

dives, diving, dived

to jump head first, usually into water

diver divers

1 someone who dives
2 someone wearing special equipment who works under water

divide

divides, dividing, divided

to share between; to split up

division

separating something into parts (÷)

divorce divorces

when a husband and wife decide to end their marriage

Diwali

the Hindu festival of lights

dizzy

dizzier, dizziest

unsteady; feeling as if you are spinning round

dock docks

1 the place where boats are loaded and unloaded
2 the place where a prisoner stands in a court of law

doctor doctors

a person who looks after people's health

document documents

written information (especially official information) on paper or on a computer

dodge

dodges, dodging, dodged

to move quickly from one side to the other; to avoid

doe does (sounds like 'no')

a female deer or rabbit

dog dogs

a hairy animal that barks and is often kept as a pet

doll dolls

a toy that looks like a small person

dollar dollars

a form of money used in some countries (for example, America and Canada)

dolphin dolphins

a large mammal that lives in the sea

dome domes

a rounded roof on a large building

domino dominoes

a piece of plastic or wood with dots or pictures on it, used in the game of dominoes

donkey donkeys

an animal like a small horse with very long ears

door doors

a flat piece of wood or other material that swings open to let you in (to a room, a wardrobe or a car, for example)

dormitory dormitories

a large room containing several beds

dose doses

the amount of medicine that you should take at one time

dot dots

a tiny round mark or point

double doubles

twice the amount

doubt

doubts, doubting, doubted

not to be sure; to question

dough

a soft mixture of flour and water

dove doves

a kind of pigeon, often white

down

1 lower; below
2 soft hair or feathers

downwards

down to a lower place

doze

dozes, dozing, dozed

to sleep lightly

dozen dozens

12; twelve

drag

drags, dragging, dragged

to pull something along the ground

dragon dragons

in stories, a winged animal that breathes fire

dragonfly dragonflies

a long insect with fine wings

drain

drains, draining, drained

to take away liquid from something

drains

the pipes that take the dirty water from buildings

drama dramas

1 a story that can be acted; a play
2 an exciting happening
3 a school subject where you learn how to act

draught draughts

a cold stream of air entering a warmer room

draughts

a game played with round pieces on a board with dark and light squares

draw

draws, drawing, drew

1 to make a picture in black or one colour only
2 a game that ends with equal scores
3 to pull something along

drawer drawers

an open box with handles on one side that fits into a piece of furniture

dreadful

very bad; terrible

a
b
c
d D
e
f
g
h
i
j
k
l
m
n
o
p
q
r
s
t
u
v
w
x
y
z

a
b
c
d D
e
f
g
h
i
j
k
l
m
n
o
p
q
r
s
t
u
v
w
x
y
z

dream

dreams, dreaming, dreamt, dreamed

to see and hear things when you are asleep

drench

drenches, drenching, drenched

to soak through with water

dress dresses

1 a piece of clothing like a skirt and top together, worn by women and girls
2 to put on your clothes
3 to clean and cover a wound

dressing gown

dressing gowns

a soft coat worn over night clothes

drift

drifts, drifting, drifted

1 to move aimlessly with the tide or with the wind
2 snow blown into a deep pile

drill drills

1 a tool for making holes
2 to make a hole

drink

drinks, drinking, drank

to swallow liquid

drip

drips, dripping, dripped

to fall in drops

drive

drives, driving, drove

to make something move (for example, a vehicle or an animal)

driver drivers

someone who drives a vehicle

drizzle

light rain falling gently

droop

droops, drooping, drooped

to hang down loosely

drop

drops, dropping, dropped

1 to fall from a height
2 one tiny spot of liquid

drought (say 'drout')

droughts

a long time when no rain falls and there is not enough water

drown

drowns, drowning, drowned

to die in water because you cannot breathe

drug drugs

1 a substance used as a medicine
2 a substance used to make people feel different (for example, a strong drink, such as beer)

drum drums

a musical instrument that is played by beating it with one or more sticks

dry

drier, driest

not wet or damp

duchess duchesses

a noblewoman of high rank; the wife or widow of a duke

duck ducks

1 a common water bird
2 to bend down quickly (so as not to be seen or hit, for example)

duel duels

a fight between two people armed with the same weapons

duet duets

a song or a piece of music for two people

duke dukes

a nobleman of high rank

dull

duller, dullest

1 not bright or shiny
2 not interesting

dumb

dumber, dumbest

unable to speak

dummy dummies

a rubber object for a baby to suck

dump

dumps, dumping, dumped

1 to put something down heavily or carelessly
2 a place where things are stored roughly or thrown away

dungeon dungeons

a prison below the ground

during

as long as something lasts

dusk

the beginning of darkness, just after sunset

dust

tiny specks of dirt, carried on the air

duster dusters

a cloth to remove dust

duties

the things people have to do (as part of their work, for example)

duvet (say '**doo**vay') duvets

a bed cover filled with soft feathers or other material

DVD DVDs

a small disk containing video or a movie

dwarf dwarves

1 a plant or an animal that is much smaller than most
2 an imaginary small person in a story

dwell

dwells, dwelling, dwelt, dwelled

to live in a certain place

dye

dyes, dyeing, dyed

to make something a certain colour by placing it in a special liquid

dynamite

a substance that can be used to make things explode

dyslexia

a certain kind of difficulty with reading and writing

a b c d D e f g h i j k l m n o p q r s t u v w x y z

eE

each
every one by itself

eager
very keen

eagle eagles
a large wild bird that kills small animals for food

ear ears
the part of the head with which you hear

earl earls
a nobleman

early
earlier, earliest
1 before the time fixed
2 near the beginning

earn
earns, earning, earned
1 to get money by working
2 to deserve

earring earrings
jewellery worn on the ear

earth
1 the world in which you live
2 the soil in which things grow

earthquake earthquakes
a time when part of the earth's surface shakes

earwig earwigs
a small insect

east
the direction from which the sun rises

Easter
Christian festival held in spring

easy
easier, easiest
simple to do; not difficult to understand

eat
eats, eating, ate
to bite, chew and swallow food

echo echoes
the sound that bounces back to you in an empty place

edge edges
the rim; the border

editor editors
1 the person in charge of a newspaper or magazine
2 a person who prepares a book or a paper for printing, or a film or a video for showing

education
learning and teaching, especially in schools, colleges and universities

eel eels
a kind of fish that looks like a snake

effect effects
what happens because of something

effort efforts

the use of all your strength or ability in trying to do something

e.g.

for example

egg eggs

the rounded object from which some creatures are hatched (for example, fish and birds)

Eid

Muslim festival at the end of Ramadan

eight

8; a number

eighteen

18; a number

eighty

80; a number

either

one or the other of two people or things

elastic

a material that will stretch and then go back to its own length

elbow elbows

the joint in the middle of the arm

elder

1 the older one of two people
2 a tree with white flowers and black berries

election elections

choosing someone by a vote

electric

using electricity

electricity

a form of energy that goes through wires and is used for heating, lighting or driving things

electronic

needing electricity and a computer chip to work

elephant elephants

a very large animal with a trunk and two tusks

eleven

11; a number

elf elves

a kind of small fairy

elm elms

a kind of large tree

e-mail e-mails

an electronic message sent using a computer

embarrass

embarrasses, embarrassing, embarrassed

to make someone feel uncomfortable

embrace

embraces, embracing, embraced

to put your arms round someone lovingly; to hug

embroider

embroiders, embroidering, embroidered

to sew patterns on cloth

a
b
c
d
e E
f
g
h
i
j
k
l
m
n
o
p
q
r
s
t
u
v
w
x
y
z

a
b
c
d
e E
f
g
h
i
j
k
l
m
n
o
p
q
r
s
t
u
v
w
x
y
z

emerald emeralds

1 a bright-green precious stone
2 the colour of this stone

emergency emergencies

something very bad that needs to be dealt with immediately

emigrate

emigrates, emigrating, emigrated

to leave one country to go to live in another

emotion emotions

something you feel strongly, such as anger or love

emperor emperors

a man who is the head of a number of countries

empire empires

many countries that are all under the same ruler

employ

employs, employing, employed

to give paid work to someone

empress empresses

a woman who is the head of a number of countries; the wife of an emperor

empty

emptier, emptiest

with nothing at all inside

enamel

1 a special kind of hard shiny paint
2 the hard covering on your teeth

enclose

encloses, enclosing, enclosed

1 to place inside
2 to surround by a fence or wall

encourage

encourages, encouraging, encouraged

to act or speak in a way that helps someone to do something

encyclopedia (sometimes spelt 'encyclopaedia') encyclopedias

a book containing facts about a lot of different things

end

ends, ending, ended

1 to finish
2 the last part of something

enemy enemies

someone you fight against

energy energies

strength to do things

engaged

1 about to be married
2 being used by someone else

engine engines

a machine that uses energy (from electricity, petrol or steam, for example) to make things move

engineer engineers

a person who plans or looks after machines, roads, buildings or bridges

enjoy

enjoys, enjoying, enjoyed

to like doing something very much

enormous

very large

enough

as many or as much as needed

enquire (sometimes spelt 'inquire')

enquires, enquiring, enquired

to ask questions

enter

enters, entering, entered

to go into or to come into

entertain

entertains, entertaining,
entertained

to put people in a good mood
by doing something to amuse
them

entertainment

entertainments

something that is done to give
pleasure to people

enthusiastic

very keen; very interested

entire

whole; complete

entrance entrances

the place where you enter; the
way in

entry entries

1 going or coming in
2 an entrance

envelope envelopes

the paper cover in which a letter
is placed

environment

environments

the air, water and land around
living things

envy

envies, envying, envied

to wish you could have what
somebody else has

equal

1 exactly the same as (=)
2 just as good as

equator

an imaginary line round the earth.
It is halfway between the North
and South Poles (see **polar**).

equipment

things that you need in order to
do something

eraser erasers

a small piece of rubber used for
getting rid of marks on paper (also
called a **rubber**)

erect

erects, erecting, erected

1 to build
2 perfectly upright

errand errands

a short journey to take a message
or to fetch something

error errors

a mistake

escalator escalators

moving stairs often found in
shopping centres and airports

a b c d **e E** f g h i j k l m n o p q r s t u v w x y z

escape

escapes, escaping, escaped

to get away; to find a way out

especially

very; more than usual

essay essays

a piece of writing on a particular subject

essential

needed; something that you must have

estate estates

1 a number of houses built together in one place
2 large piece of land belonging to one person

estimate

estimates, estimating, estimated

to guess the size or price of something

etc.

and so on

eternal

lasting for ever

even

1 flat and smooth
2 describes a number that can be divided by two (for example, 4, 6 and 8); not odd

evening evenings

the time between afternoon and night

event events

1 a happening, especially an important one
2 an item on a sports programme

eventually

at last; in the end

ever

always; at all times

evergreen evergreens

a plant that does not lose its leaves in the winter

every

each one of many

evident

easy to see; plain

evil

very bad; very wicked

ewe (say 'you') ewes

a female sheep

exact

absolutely correct; quite right

exaggerate

exaggerates, exaggerating, exaggerated

to say more than is really true

examination (exam)
examinations (exams)

a test of how good someone or something is in a particular way; a check-up

examine

examines, examining, examined

to look at something carefully

example examples

1 one thing taken out of a number of things to show what the rest are like
2 good behaviour you should copy

excellent

very good

exception exceptions

something not included with everything else

exchange

exchanges, exchanging, exchanged

1 to change for something else
2 a building where telephone lines are connected

excite

excites, exciting, excited

to give strong and often pleasant feelings

exclaim

exclaims, exclaiming, exclaimed

to shout out suddenly

excursion excursions

a journey for pleasure

excuse (sounds like 'loose') excuses

a reason for not doing what you should have done

excuse (sounds like 'news')
excuses, excusing, excused

to pardon; to forgive

execute

executes, executing, executed

to put to death

exercise exercises

movement that helps keep you fit (for example, walking or running)

exhibition exhibitions

a display; a show (for example, of pictures)

exist

exists, existing, existed

to live; to be

exit exits

the way out of a place

expand

expands, expanding, expanded

to grow larger; to spread out

expect

expects, expecting, expected

to think that something will happen

expedition expeditions

a special journey to a place to find out more about it

expensive

costing a lot of money

experiment experiments

a test done on something to find out more about it

expert experts

a person who is very good at something or knows a lot about something

explain

explains, explaining, explained

to say clearly how something happened or what something is about so that people understand

explode

explodes, exploding, exploded

to burst or blow up with a loud noise

explore

explores, exploring, explored

to travel around; to search or examine a place thoroughly to find out more about it

a
b
c
d
e
f F
g
h
i
j
k
l
m
n
o
p
q
r
s
t
u
v
w
x
y
z

export

exports, exporting, exported

to send goods out of a country

express

expresses, expressing, expressed

1 to state your thoughts and ideas or show your feelings
2 travelling more quickly than usual

extend

extends, extending, extended

to stretch out; to make longer or larger

extinct

no longer existing

extra

1 in addition to
2 more than is needed or usual

extraordinary

very strange; unusual

extreme

1 farthest away
2 very great indeed

eye eyes

1 the part of the head with which you see
2 the hole in a needle

eyebrow eyebrows

the line of hair that grows on your forehead above each eye

eyelid eyelids

the skin that covers your eyes when you blink or close them

eyesight

the ability to see

fable fables

a story or legend, often about animals, that teaches you something

face faces

1 the front part of the head
2 the front of an object
3 one side of a shape
4 to turn towards something

fact facts

something that is true

factory factories

a place where things are made by machinery

fade

fades, fading, faded

1 to lose colour; to get dimmer
2 to grow weaker

fail

fails, failing, failed

1 not to do something that you are expected to do
2 not to pass an exam

faint

fainter, faintest

1 not clear; not easy to see
2 to lose your senses and to stop being conscious for a short time

fair fairs

1 an open-air entertainment;
a market
2 light in colour; not dark
3 just; treating every person the
same
4 neither good nor bad; quite good

fairground fairgrounds

an open area where fairs are held

fairy fairies

an imaginary person, often tiny,
who can use magic to do special
things

faith faiths

belief in somebody or something

faithful

true; to be trusted

fall

falls, falling, fell

to drop; to come down; to move
lower down

false

falser, falsest

not true; not real

familiar

well-known to you

family families

a group of people who are related
(for example, a father, a mother
and their child or children)

famine famines

being without food for a long time

famous

well known because of what you
have done

fan fans

1 an instrument that makes air
move and keeps you cool
2 a person who is very interested
in something or someone (for
example, a football team or a
pop singer)

fancy

fancier, fanciest

1 decorated; not plain
2 to want

fang fangs

a long sharp tooth found in some
animals and snakes

far

farther, farthest

not near; a long way away

fare fares

money paid for a journey

farm farms

land used for growing crops and
keeping animals

farmer farmers

a person who owns or looks after
a farm

fashion

up-to-date clothes and styles

fast

faster, fastest

1 very quick; speedy
2 a time without food
3 fixed

fasten

fastens, fastening, fastened

to tie or join things together

fat

fatter, fattest

1 very big all round; not thin
2 the grease from animals and plants that is used for cooking
3 the greasy part of meat

fatal

causing death

fate fates

what is going to happen or is likely to happen in the future

father fathers

a male parent

fault faults

1 a mistake in the way something was made
2 something you do wrong that makes a bad thing happen

favour favours

something good you do for someone

favourite favourites

the one that you like better than any of the others

fawn fawns

1 a young deer
2 a light-brown colour

fear

fears, fearing, feared

to be afraid of; to be frightened that something bad might happen

feast feasts

a special meal for lots of people to eat together

feather feathers

one of the light fluffy things that cover a bird's body and wings

feeble

feebler, feeblest

weak; with no strength

feed

feeds, feeding, fed

to give food to

feel

feels, feeling, felt

1 to touch something to find out what it is like
2 to have a feeling (for example, sadness or happiness)

fellow fellows

a man or boy

felt

thick woolly cloth

female females

a person or an animal that can one day be a mother; a girl or a woman

feminine

to do with girls or women

fence fences

1 something built of wood or metal to separate one area from another
2 to fight with swords as a sport

fern ferns

a type of plant with feathery leaves but no flowers

ferret ferrets

a small furry animal

ferry ferries

a boat that carries people and cars across water

festival festivals

a special occasion where large numbers of people enjoy themselves together

fetch

fetches, fetching, fetched

to go and get; to bring back what you were sent for

fever fevers

an illness that makes the body hot

few

fewer, fewest

not many

fibre fibres

a thread-like substance usually used to make into something

fiction

a story about people or happenings that are not real

fiddle fiddles

a violin

fidget

fidgets, fidgeting, fidgeted

to be restless; to wriggle about

field fields

a piece of land with a hedge, fence or wall around it, where animals are kept or crops are grown

fierce

fiercer, fiercest

wild; cruel; violent

fifteen

15; a number

fifty

50; a number

fig figs

a sweet fruit full of tiny seeds

fight fights

a struggle or battle between two or more people

figure figures

1 number used in mathematics
2 a shape
3 a person; the shape of the human body

file files

1 an instrument with a rough edge for making things smooth
2 a line of people one behind the other
3 a folder where papers and documents are kept in an office or on a computer

fill

fills, filling, filled

to make full

film films

1 a very thin covering
2 a story shown in a cinema or on television; a movie

filthy

filthier, filthiest

very dirty

fin fins

one of the thin flat parts of a fish that stick out from its body and help it to swim

a
b
c
d
e
f F
g
h
i
j
k
l
m
n
o
p
q
r
s
t
u
v
w
x
y
z

final finals

1 the end; the last
2 the last match in a competition, which decides the winner

finch finches

a kind of small bird

find

finds, finding, found

to come across something, usually something that you have been looking for

(also see **found**)

fine

finer, finest

1 when the weather is pleasant
2 very good; excellent
3 a sum of money paid as a punishment for breaking the law

finger fingers

one of the four longest parts of the hand

finish

finishes, finishing, finished

to complete; to end

fir firs

an evergreen tree with cones

fire fires

1 the flames and heat that you see when something is burning
2 to shoot a gun

fire-fighter fire-fighters

a person whose job it is to prevent or put out fires and rescue people from them

firework fireworks

a container filled with powder that makes pretty coloured flames and sparks when lit

firm

firmer, firmest

1 fixed; not easy to move when you push it
2 a group of people running a business

first

1 coming before everyone or everything else
2 at the very beginning

first aid

helping someone who has been hurt or is ill, before a doctor comes

fish fish, fishes

1 an animal that lives and breathes in water
2 to try to catch fish to eat or as a sport

fisherman fishermen

a person who catches fish

fist fists

the hand and fingers closed tightly together

fit

fitter, fittest

1 in good health; well and strong
2 suitable
3 to be the right size for

five

5; a number

fix

fixes, fixing, fixed

1 to put in place firmly
2 to put right

fizzy

fizzier, fizziest

with a lot of bubbles

flag flags

a piece of cloth with a special pattern and colours that is the special sign of something (a country or a club, for example)

flake flakes

a small thin piece of something

flame flames

the part of a fire that is bright and blazing

flannel flannels

a soft cloth that soaks up water, used for washing your face or body

flap

flaps, flapping, flapped

1 to move up and down (for example, like a bird's wings)
2 a piece that hangs down over something

flare

flares, flaring, flared

to blaze up suddenly

flash flashes

a beam of light that comes and goes quickly

flask flasks

short for **vacuum flask**

flat

flatter, flattest

1 level; smooth; not sloping or bumpy
2 a set of rooms all on one floor, where people live
3 a sound that is just below the correct note in music

flatter

flatters, flattering, flattered

to say that someone is better than they really are

flavour flavours

the taste of something

flaw flaws

a fault; a weak place

flea fleas

a tiny jumping insect that bites people and animals

flee

flees, fleeing, fled

to go away quickly; to run from trouble or danger

fleece

1 the wool of a sheep or a goat
2 a lightweight jacket that keeps you warm

fleet

a number of ships together

flesh

the soft part of the body that covers the bones

a b c d e f F g h i j k l m n o p q r s t u v w x y z

a
b
c
d
e

f F

g
h
i
j
k
l
m
n
o
p
q
r
s
t
u
v
w
x
y
z

flight flights

1 flying
2 escaping

fling

flings, flinging, flung

to throw something away from you

flint flints

a kind of very hard stone

float

floats, floating, floated

to stay on the surface of water or be held up by the air

flock flocks

a number of animals of the same sort together, especially sheep or birds

flood floods

when water overflows from rivers and lakes onto roads and fields

floor floors

1 the part of a room you walk on
2 one level in a building

florist florists

a person who sells flowers

flour

wheat that has been crushed into a powder which is used for baking

flow

flows, flowing, flowed

to move along smoothly, like running water

flower flowers

the part of a plant that has coloured petals and produces seeds or fruit

flu

an illness like a very bad cold that makes you shiver and ache all over

fluff

small soft pieces (for example, of cloth) that can fly about and catch dust

flute flutes

a high-pitched metal or wooden musical instrument played by blowing

flutter

flutters, fluttering, fluttered

to make quick light movements (for example, like a bird's wings)

fly

flies, flying, flew

1 to move through the air, especially with wings or in a plane
2 a kind of small insect with wings

foal foals

a young horse

foam

bubbles on the top of a liquid

fog

air that is thick with a mist made of very small water drops

fold

folds, folding, folded

to bend something so that one part covers another

folder folders

1 a cardboard cover for papers
2 a file for storing information on a computer

folk

people

follow

follows, following, followed

1 to go after; to come after
2 to be able to understand something you hear or read

fond

fonder, fondest

liking someone or something very much

food

what people, animals and plants take in to keep them alive

fool

fools, fooling, fooled

1 to trick somebody
2 a person who behaves in a silly way

foolish

slightly stupid; silly

foot feet

1 the part of the leg you stand on
2 a measure of length (the same as about 30 centimetres)

football

1 a game played by two teams kicking a ball
2 a special ball for playing football

footwear

things worn on the feet (boots, shoes and socks, for example)

forbid

forbids, forbidding, forbade

to tell somebody not to do something

force

forces, forcing, forced

1 to make somebody do something
2 strength

forecast

forecasts, forecasting, forecasted

to say what is likely to happen

forehead foreheads

the part of the head between the hair and the eyes

foreign

belonging to another country

forest forests

a large area of woodland

forge

forges, forging, forged

to copy someone's handwriting, painting or signature and pretend that it is really theirs

forget

forgets, forgetting, forgot

1 not to remember
2 to leave something behind

forgive

forgives, forgiving, forgave

to stop being angry with someone even though they have done something wrong

fork forks

1 a small tool with long thin spikes for eating with
2 a large tool with a long handle and long thin spikes, used in the garden
3 where a road divides into two

a b c d e f F g h i j k l m n o p q r s t u v w x y z

form forms

1 the shape of something
2 a printed paper with spaces for you to write things in
3 a class in a school

fort forts

a strong building built to protect people from attack

fortnight

a period of two weeks

fortunate

lucky

fortune fortunes

1 good or bad luck
2 a lot of money

forty

40; a number

forward (or **forwards**)

towards the front; ahead of

fossil fossils

the mark or remains of a creature or plant found inside rocks

foster

fosters, fostering, fostered

to bring up a child who is not your own

found

founds, founding, founded

to start something, such as a hospital or a school

(also see **find**)

fountain fountains

a fixed device for throwing a thin stream of water into the air

four

4; a number

fourteen

14; a number

fowl fowl, fowls

a bird, especially one kept for its meat and eggs

fox foxes

a wild animal like a dog with a long thick tail

fraction fractions

a part of something

fragment fragments

a small piece from something larger

frame frames

a border placed round a picture

framework frameworks

a basic structure or frame on which something is made

freckle freckles

one of the tiny light-brown marks found on the skin of some people

free

1 able to do as you wish
2 given away for nothing

freeze

freezes, freezing, froze

to make or become very hard and cold; to turn into ice

freezer freezers

a refrigerator that keeps things so cold that they stay frozen

frequent

happening often

fresh

fresher, freshest

1 new; newly gathered; just made
2 not tired
3 (of water) not salty

fridge fridges

short for **refrigerator**

friend friends

somebody you like and can trust and enjoy doing things with

fright

sudden fear

frill frills

a decoration round the edge

fringe fringes

1 short hair brushed forward over the forehead
2 a border of loose threads (for example, used to decorate a rug)

frisky

friskier, friskiest

lively; jumping with pleasure

frog frogs

a small jumping animal that can live on land and in water

front

the part facing forwards

frost frosts

white powdery ice seen in very cold weather

froth

bubbles on top of a liquid; foam

frown

frowns, frowning, frowned

to wrinkle the forehead to show that you are annoyed or puzzled

frozen

very cold; made into ice

fruit fruit, fruits

the part of certain plants where the seeds are found; many fruits are good to eat (for example, strawberries, pineapples and oranges)

fry

fries, frying, fried

to cook in boiling fat or oil in a pan

fudge

a kind of soft brown toffee

fuel fuels

anything that can be burned to give heat or light

full

fuller, fullest

unable to hold anything more

fun

enjoyable, amusing and lively

fund funds

a collection of money for something special

funeral funerals

the ceremony held when someone dies

a b c d e **f F** g h i j k l m n o p q r s t u v w x y z

a
b
c
d
e
f
g G
h
i
j
k
l
m
n
o
p
q
r
s
t
u
v
w
x
y
z

funnel funnels

1 the chimney on a ship or an engine
2 a tube with a wide mouth (used to pour liquids, for example)

funny
funnier, funniest

1 amusing; making you laugh
2 strange; odd

fur furs

the soft hairy covering of some animals

furious

very angry

furnace furnaces

a covered fire that melts metals

furniture

chairs, tables, beds and other such objects used around your home

furry
furrier, furriest

having a soft hairy covering

further furthest

at a greater distance; beyond

fuse fuses

1 a piece of material that is lit to set off an explosion
2 the part of an electrical plug or piece of equipment that stops the current flowing if necessary

fuss

an excited state, usually about something quite small

future

the time yet to come

gG

gable gables

the pointed end wall of a building

gadget gadgets

a small object that does something useful

gag
gags, gagging, gagged

to cover the mouth to prevent a person from speaking

gain gains

1 a profit that is made
2 to get or win something

gale gales

a very strong wind

galleon galleons

a Spanish sailing-ship from long ago

gallery galleries

1 a high platform, often with seats, in a large hall (a cinema, a theatre or a church, for example)
2 a building or a large room used for showing pictures or sculptures

galley galleys

1 a ship's kitchen
2 a kind of low sailing-ship with many oars, from long ago

gallon gallons

a measure of liquid equal to about four and a half litres or eight pints

gallop

gallops, galloping, galloped

to move very fast on four legs, like a horse

gamble

gambles, gambling, gambled

to play games for money; to take the risk of losing something

game games

1 something that you play; a sport
2 wild animals or birds that are hunted for food

gander ganders

a male goose

gang gangs

a group of people doing something together

gangway gangways

1 a pathway between rows of seats
2 a bridge placed between a ship and the dock

gaol (say 'jail') gaols

a prison. The word may also be spelt jail.

gap gaps

an opening between two places or things

gape

gapes, gaping, gaped

to open wide

garage garages

1 a place where cars are kept
2 a place where cars are repaired

garbage

rubbish; waste; things to be thrown out

garden gardens

land where flowers, fruit or vegetables are grown

garment garments

a piece of clothing

gas gases

1 something like air, which is neither liquid nor solid
2 a kind of gas that burns, used for heating and cooking

gash gashes

a long deep cut

gasp

gasps, gasping, gasped

to breathe in very quickly, often in surprise

gate gates

a kind of door in a wall or a fence

gather

gathers, gathering, gathered

1 to collect together
2 to pick flowers, fruit or vegetables

gaze

gazes, gazing, gazed

to look for a long time; to stare steadily

gazelle gazelles

a kind of small deer found in Africa and Asia

gear gears

1 a set of wheels with teeth that make an engine turn
2 the clothes and equipment you need for something (to play a sport, for example)

gem gems

a precious stone that is used for jewellery (for example, a diamond)

general

1 usual; often done
2 an army officer of high rank

generous

kind; likely to give away freely

genius geniuses

a person who is very clever

gentle

gentler, gentlest

soft; not rough; quiet and kind

gentleman gentlemen

1 a man who is well-mannered
2 a polite word for a man

genuine

real; true

geography

knowledge about the earth and its people; geography is sometimes a school subject

geology

knowledge about rocks and how they are made

gerbil gerbils

a small animal like a mouse, often kept as a pet

germ germs

a tiny living thing that can make you ill

ghost ghosts

the image of a dead person that some people see or can feel

giant giants

1 a huge person (for example, in a fairy story)
2 anything that is much larger than usual

giddy

giddier, giddiest

dizzy; when everything seems to be going round and round

gift gifts

a present

gigantic

very big; enormous

giggle

giggles, giggling, giggled

to laugh quietly in a foolish way

gills

the openings in a fish's head by which it breathes

ginger

1 a kind of hot flavouring used in cooking
2 a reddish-brown colour

giraffe giraffes

an African wild animal with a very long neck and long legs

girl girls

a female child or young woman

give

gives, giving, gave

to hand over to someone else

glad

happy; pleased

glance

glances, glancing, glanced

to look at something quickly and then look away

glare

glares, glaring, glared

1 to stare at in anger
2 unpleasant brightness

glass

1 a hard material that you can usually see through
2 a cup that is without a handle and is made of glass

glasses

two pieces of glass or plastic worn over your eyes to help you to see better

gleam

gleams, gleaming, gleamed

to shine faintly

glide

glides, gliding, glided

to move along very smoothly

glider gliders

a kind of aeroplane that glides through the air without an engine

glimmer

a faint light that can hardly be seen

glimpse glimpses

a very short look; a glance

glitter

glitters, glittering, glittered

to reflect rays of light; to sparkle

globe globes

1 an object like a ball
2 a ball with a map of the world drawn on it

gloomy

gloomier, gloomiest

1 dark and dismal
2 sad and serious

glory glories

the great respect shown towards a person who has done something important

gloss

brightness on the surface of something

glove gloves

a covering for the hand with a separate place for each finger

glow

glows, glowing, glowed

to shine with a soft light; to burn without flame

glue

something used to stick things together

glum

sad and unhappy

glutton gluttons

a person who eats too much

a
b
c
d
e
f
g G
h
i
j
k
l
m
n
o
p
q
r
s
t
u
v
w
x
y
z

gnash (say 'nash')

gnashes, gnashing, gnashed

to grind your teeth together because you are angry or in trouble

gnat (say 'nat') **gnats**

a tiny winged insect that bites

gnaw (say 'naw')

gnaws, gnawing, gnawed

to wear away by using the teeth; to eat by scraping away

gnome (say 'nome') **gnomes**

a dwarf or goblin that is supposed to live under the ground

go

goes, going, went

to move away; to leave

goal goals

1 a place you aim at in games (in football and hockey, for example)
2 the score made when the ball goes into the goal
3 something you hope to do in the future

goat goats

a farm animal with small horns

gobble

gobbles, gobbling, gobbled

to eat greedily and noisily

goblin goblins

a kind of wicked fairy

God

the being who is above all others and to whom people pray

gold

a yellow precious metal

golden

1 looking like gold
2 made of gold

goldfish goldfish

a small orange fish, often kept as a pet

golf

a game played on a large stretch of land with special clubs and a small ball

good

better, best

1 right; true
2 kind
3 well-behaved

goodbye

something you say to people when you leave them

goods

things that are bought, sold and owned

goose geese

a bird like a large duck

gooseberry gooseberries

a green fruit that grows on a small prickly bush

gorgeous

splendid; magnificent; very beautiful

gorilla gorillas

a type of huge monkey that lives in the jungle

gospel gospels

the teachings of Jesus Christ

gossip

gossips, gossiping, gossiped

1 to talk for a long time about unimportant things, often about other people
2 a person who tells stories, usually hurtful, about others

govern

governs, governing, governed

to be in control of; to rule over (for example, a country)

government governments

the people in charge of a country

gown gowns

a dress

grab

grabs, grabbing, grabbed

to snatch; to grasp quickly

grace graces

1 a prayer before or after a meal
2 a beautiful way of moving
3 a kind way of behaving

grade grades

1 a level; size; quality
2 your mark in an exam
3 to put into groups (for example, according to size)

gradual

little by little

grain grains

1 the small hard seed of a cereal plant, used for food
2 a tiny piece of sand or soil
3 the lines in wood

gram grams

a small unit of mass

grammar

the rules of a language

grand

grander, grandest

very large and fine

grandchild

the child of a son or daughter

grandfather (granddad, grandpa) grandfathers (granddads, grandpas)

the father of your father or mother

grandmother (grandma, granny) grandmothers (grandmas, grannies)

the mother of your father or mother

granite

a very hard rock often used for buildings and monuments

grant

grants, granting, granted

to give; to allow

grape grapes

a small juicy fruit with green or purple skin, which grows in a bunch

grapefruit grapefruits

a yellow fruit like a large orange

graph graphs

a kind of diagram or chart that shows information

a
b
c
d
e
f
g G
h
i
j
k
l
m
n
o
p
q
r
s
t
u
v
w
x
y
z

grasp
grasps, grasping, grasped
1 to hold firmly
2 to understand what you have been told

grass grasses
the common green plant that grows in fields and gardens

grasshopper grasshoppers
an insect that jumps using its strong back legs

grate
grates, grating, grated
1 to rub something into little pieces using a rough surface
2 the place where a fire burns

grateful
thankful; feeling gratitude

grater graters
an instrument with rough points used to grate things (cheese, for example)

gratitude
warm feelings towards someone who has been helpful or kind

grave graves
1 a burial place in the ground
2 serious

gravel
small pieces of stone

gravity
the force that pulls objects towards the earth

gravy
a brown liquid eaten with meat

graze
grazes, grazing, grazed
1 to rub away the skin
2 to feed on grass

grease
1 animal fat
2 thick oil used to make machinery run smoothly

great
greater, greatest
1 big
2 important
3 very good

greedy
greedier, greediest
always wanting more; never satisfied

green
greener, greenest
1 the colour of grass
2 an area of grass
3 not harmful to nature

greenhouse greenhouses
a building with glass walls and roof in which plants are grown

greet
greets, greeting, greeted
to welcome with words and actions

grey
greyer, greyest
a colour halfway between black and white

grief
sorrow; deep sadness (felt when someone dies, for example)

grill
grills, grilling, grilled

1 to cook food by putting it very close to the heat (on a barbecue, for example)
2 the part of a cooker where you can grill food

grim
grimmer, grimmest

stern; severe; fierce

grin grins
a wide smile

grind
grinds, grinding, ground

1 to rub something until it becomes powder
2 to sharpen by rubbing the edge of something (a tool, for example)

grip
grips, gripping, gripped

to grasp tightly

groan
groans, groaning, groaned

to make a low sad sound, usually when hurt or ill

groom grooms
1 a person who looks after horses
2 to brush and clean a horse
3 short for **bridegroom**

groove grooves
a narrow channel cut into something

ground
1 the surface of the earth; land
2 a place for playing certain outdoor games

group groups
a number of people, animals or things together

grouse
grouses, grousing, groused

1 to complain; to grumble
2 a plump bird found especially on the Scottish moors

grow
grows, growing, grew

1 to get bigger
2 to look after plants so that they get bigger

growl
growls, growling, growled

to show anger by snarling like a dog

grub grubs
an insect before it has grown wings or legs (for example, a caterpillar)

grubby
grubbier, grubbiest

dirty

gruff
gruffer, gruffest

having a rough voice

grumble
grumbles, grumbling, grumbled

to complain, not loudly but often

grunt grunts
a noise like the sound made by a pig

guard
guards, guarding, guarded

1 to keep safe
2 a person whose job it is to protect something or someone
3 a person in charge of a train

a
b
c
d
e
f
g G
h
i
j
k
l
m
n
o
p
q
r
s
t
u
v
w
x
y
z

a
b
c
d
e
f
g G
h
i
j
k
l
m
n
o
p
q
r
s
t
u
v
w
x
y
z

guardian guardians

someone who looks after another person, especially when taking the place of a parent

guess

guesses, guessing, guessed

to say what you think might be correct without really knowing

guest guests

1 a visitor to someone's house
2 a person staying in a hotel

guide guides

1 a person who shows you a place or shows you the way
2 a Guide is a member of the Guides, a club that provides adventure activities for girls
3 **guidebook** a book giving information about a place
4 **guide dog** a dog trained to lead a blind person

guilt

1 having done wrong
2 the feeling of having done wrong

guinea pig guinea pigs

a small furry animal with no tail that is usually kept as a pet

guitar guitars

a musical instrument with six strings, played by plucking the strings

gulf gulfs

a large bay

gull gulls

a kind of common sea bird

gulp

gulps, gulping, gulped

to swallow greedily and noisily

gum

1 a substance used to stick things together
2 **gums** the part of the mouth round the roots of the teeth
3 **chewing gum** a chewy sweet

gun guns

a weapon that fires bullets

guppy guppies

a type of small, brightly-coloured fish

gurgle

gurgles, gurgling, gurgled

to make a bubbling noise like water leaving a container

gush

gushes, gushing, gushed

to flow out quickly in large amounts

gust gusts

a sudden wind

gutter gutters

a channel for water along the edge of a road or roof

guy guys

1 a model of Guy Fawkes, burnt on a bonfire on 5 November
2 a man

gymnast gymnasts

a person skilled in gymnastics

gymnastics (gym)

exercises for the body

hH

habit habits

something you do a lot without thinking about it much

haddock haddock

a sea fish used as food

haggard

looking tired, thin and ill

hail

frozen drops of rain

hair hairs

a thread-like covering that grows on the head and body

hairdresser hairdressers

a person who cuts and arranges hair

half halves

one of two equal parts of a thing

hall halls

1 a very large room where people meet
2 the room inside the front door of your home

halo halos

1 a ring of light (round the sun or moon, for example)
2 the circle painted or drawn round the heads of holy people in pictures

halt

halts, halting, halted

to stop

halter halters

a special strap used for leading a horse

halve

halves, halving, halved

to divide into two equal parts

ham

salted or smoked meat from a pig's leg

hamburger (burger)
hamburgers (burgers)

a portion of minced meat fried and eaten in a bread roll

hammer hammers

a tool with a metal head used to hit nails (into wood, for example)

hammock hammocks

a hanging bed held up by ropes

hamper hampers

1 a large basket with a lid
2 to make it difficult for you to do something

hamster hamsters

a small animal like a large mouse, often kept as a pet

hand hands

1 the part of the arm below the wrist
2 a pointer on a clock
3 to pass something to someone

handbag handbags

a bag carried in the hand

a
b
c
d
e
f
g
h H
i
j
k
l
m
n
o
p
q
r
s
t
u
v
w
x
y
z

a
b
c
d
e
f
g
h H
i
j
k
l
m
n
o
p
q
r
s
t
u
v
w
x
y
z

handicap handicaps

something that keeps you back;
a disadvantage

handkerchief (hanky)
handkerchiefs (hankies)

a small piece of cloth for wiping
your nose on

handle

handles, handling, handled

1 to touch with the hand
2 the part of something that you
   hold in your hand

handlebars

the part of a bicycle that you hold
to steer it

handrail handrails

a rail to hold on to for safety

handsome

more handsome, most handsome

good-looking

handy

handier, handiest

useful

hang

hangs, hanging, hung

to fasten something at the top so
that it swings

hanger hangers

a piece of wood, plastic or wire
specially shaped to hang clothes on

Hanukkah

the Jewish festival of lights

happen

happens, happening, happened

to take place; to occur

happy

happier, happiest

feeling very pleased; glad

harass

harasses, harassing, harassed

to annoy; to cause difficulties

harbour harbours

a place of shelter for boats

hard

harder, hardest

1 difficult to do
2 tough; firm; not soft

hardly

scarcely; only just

hardy

hardier, hardiest

strong; able to bear pain; able to
live in difficult conditions

hare hares

an animal like a large rabbit, with
very long ears

harm

damage; injury

harness harnesses

the straps used to control
something (for example, a horse)

harp harps

a musical instrument that is played
by plucking the strings

harpoon harpoons

a spear used for catching large fish

harsh

harsher, harshest

rough; severe; unkind

harvest harvests

1 a crop of food to be gathered in
2 the time when this is done

haste

speed; quickness; hurry

hat hats

a covering worn on the head

hatch

hatches, hatching, hatched

to be born from an egg

hatchet hatchets

a small axe

hate

hates, hating, hated

to dislike very much

haul

hauls, hauling, hauled

to drag; to pull with effort

haunted

often visited by a ghost

have

has, having, had

to possess; to own

hawk hawks

a large bird that hunts small birds or animals for food

hay

dried grass used as animal food

haze

very light mist or thin cloud

hazel hazels

1 a small tree with brown nuts that you can eat
2 a light-brown colour

head heads

1 the part of the body above the neck
2 the person in charge
3 the front part or top of something

headache headaches

a pain in the head

headphones

things you put over your ears to listen to music or speech without other people hearing

headscarf headscarves

a piece of cloth worn over the head, often covering the hair

headteacher headteachers

the teacher in charge of a school

heal

heals, healing, healed

to get well again after being hurt

health

1 the state of your body or mind
2 being well; being free from illness; fitness

heap heaps

things placed one on top of another untidily; a pile

hear

hears, hearing, heard

to catch the sound of; to listen to

a b c d e f g

h H

i j k l m n o p q r s t u v w x y z

a
b
c
d
e
f
g
h H
i
j
k
l
m
n
o
p
q
r
s
t
u
v
w
x
y
z

hearing aid hearing aids

a device worn behind the ear to help a person who cannot hear properly

heart hearts

1 the part of the body that pumps the blood round the body
2 a shape with two rounded parts at the top and a sharp point at the bottom
3 one of the four kinds in a pack of playing cards

heat

1 warmth; being hot
2 one of the races leading to a final

heather

a small plant with purple or white flowers that grows on moorlands

heave

heaves, heaving, heaved

1 to pull strongly
2 to lift something and then throw it

heaven

the place where God is said to live; perfect happiness

heavy

heavier, heaviest

having great weight

hedge hedges

small bushes or trees grown in lines to separate fields or gardens

hedgehog hedgehogs

a small animal with prickles on its back that rolls itself into a ball when in danger

heel heels

the back part of the foot

height

the distance from top to bottom; how tall you are

heir heirs

a person who receives a dead person's property

helicopter helicopters

an aircraft that flies using large pieces of metal which go round and round very fast on its roof

hell

the opposite of **heaven**

helmet helmets

a hard hat worn to protect the head from injury

help

helps, helping, helped

to do something for another person

helpless

unable to do things for yourself

hem hems

an edge of cloth that has been turned over and stitched

hemisphere hemispheres

1 one of the two halves of the world
2 half of a sphere

hen hens

1 a kind of bird kept on a farm. Its eggs and meat are used for food.
2 a female bird

herb herbs

a plant that is grown for use in cooking, to flavour food

herd herds

a large number of the same kind of animals living together (cows, for example)

hermit hermits

a person who lives on his or her own, usually in a lonely place

hero heroes

1 a person who acts with great bravery
2 the main character in a story

herring herring, herrings

a sea fish used for food

hesitate

hesitates, hesitating, hesitated

to pause before you do something because you are not sure

hexagon hexagons

a flat shape that has six sides

hibernate

hibernates, hibernating, hibernated

to sleep through the winter as some animals do

hiccup hiccups

a sudden noise in your throat, which you cannot control

hide

hides, hiding, hid

1 to keep something in a secret place
2 to go where you cannot be found

hideous

terrible to look at; ugly; frightening

high

higher, highest

tall; well above the ground

highwayman highwaymen

a man from long ago who stopped travellers and robbed them

hijab hijabs

headscarf worn by Muslim women

hill hills

a high piece of land, often with steep sides

hinder

hinders, hindering, hindered

to make it difficult for you to do something

Hindu Hindus

a follower of the religion Hinduism, especially in India

hinge hinges

a moving joint that allows a door or window to open and close easily

hint hints

a suggestion that is not made in the most direct way

hip hips

the place where the legs join the body

hippopotamus (hippo) hippopotamuses (hippos)

a large African wild animal that likes to wade in mud

a
b
c
d
e
f
g
h H
i
j
k
l
m
n
o
p
q
r
s
t
u
v
w
x
y
z

a
b
c
d
e
f
g
h H
i
j
k
l
m
n
o
p
q
r
s
t
u
v
w
x
y
z

hire

hires, hiring, hired

to borrow something for a short time and pay for its use

hiss

hisses, hissing, hissed

to push air sharply through the teeth

history

what happened in the past; history is sometimes a school subject

hit

hits, hitting, hit

to strike or knock something or someone

hive hives

the place where bees live

hoarse

hoarser, hoarsest

having a rough harsh voice

hobby hobbies

something you like doing in your spare time

hockey

a game played by two teams with curved sticks and a ball

hoe hoes

a tool used for breaking up the soil and taking out weeds

hold

holds, holding, held

1 to keep in your hand
2 to have inside; to contain
3 the part of a ship where you store things

hole holes

an opening; a gap

holiday holidays

a time when you are free from work or school and can go away

hollow

empty; with nothing inside

holly

a green tree or bush with prickly leaves and red berries

holy

holier, holiest

connected with a god

home homes

the place where you live

honest

to be trusted; truthful

honey

a sweet food made by bees

honour

1 great respect
2 fame

hood hoods

1 the part of some sweatshirts or coats that you can pull up over your head
2 a folding cover for a baby's pram or for a car

hoof hooves

the hard part of the foot of some animals (for example, horses)

hook hooks

a bent and pointed piece of metal, wood or plastic, used to hold or catch things

hoop hoops

a ring of wood, plastic or metal

hoot hoots

1 the sound made by a car horn
2 the sound made by an owl

hop

hops, hopping, hopped

to jump up and down on one foot

hope

hopes, hoping, hoped

to wish and believe that something you want will happen

hopeless

1 giving no reason for hope
2 very bad

horizon

the line where the sky and the earth seem to touch

horizontal

lying flat; parallel to the horizon; the opposite to vertical

horn horns

1 a sharp bone that grows out of the head of some animals
2 a musical instrument that you blow through
3 the device on a vehicle that makes a special warning noise

horrible

very unpleasant

horrid

dreadful; causing fear

horror horrors

something very frightening or terrible

horse horses

a large animal often used to ride on and sometimes to pull vehicles

hose hoses

a tube through which water can be directed

hospital hospitals

a place where sick people are cared for

hospitality

the welcome shown to guests

host hosts

a person who invites others to his or her house as guests

hostile

very unfriendly

hot

hotter, hottest

very warm

hot dog hot dogs

a long sausage in a bread roll

hotel hotels

a building where you can pay to stay the night

hound hounds

a type of dog

hour hours

a length of time of 60 minutes; there are 24 hours in one day

house houses

a building in which people live

hover

hovers, hovering, hovered

to stay in the air above or near a place or thing

a b c d e f g h H i j k l m n o p q r s t u v w x y z

a
b
c
d
e
f
g
h H
i
j
k
l
m
n
o
p
q
r
s
t
u
v
w
x
y
z

hovercraft hovercrafts

a vehicle that travels over water on a big cushion filled with air

howl howls

a long loud cry

hub hubs

the centre part of a wheel

huff huffs

a bad mood

hug

hugs, hugging, hugged

to hold tightly in the arms

huge

huger, hugest

very large

hum

hums, humming, hummed

1 to make the sound of a tune with your lips closed
2 a noise like that made by bees

human humans

1 a person
2 to do with people

humour

1 finding or making things funny
2 mood

hump humps

1 a large lump on the back (for example, on the back of a camel)
2 a mound of earth

hundred

100; a number

hunger

a great need, usually for food

hunt

hunts, hunting, hunted

1 to look very carefully for something
2 to try to catch or kill wild animals

hurricane hurricanes

a storm with a very strong wind

hurry

hurries, hurrying, hurried

to move very quickly; to rush

hurt

hurts, hurting, hurt

1 to make someone feel pain
2 to feel pain

husband husbands

a married man

hut huts

a small building or shed, usually made of wood

hutch hutches

a small cage of wood and metal used as a home for small pets (for example, rabbits)

hyacinth hyacinths

a sweet-smelling spring flower grown from a bulb

hyena hyenas

an African or Asian animal like a large dog that hunts other animals

hymn hymns

a religious song of praise or thanks

 **iI**

ice
frozen water

iceberg icebergs
a very large piece of ice floating in the sea

ice cream
a frozen food that is creamy, soft and sweet

ice lolly (lolly)
ice lollies (lollies)
flavoured ice or ice cream on a stick

icicle icicles
a pointed piece of ice that hangs down from something

icing
a sweet mixture sometimes spread over cakes and buns

idea ideas
a thought; something in the mind

ideal
just what is needed; the best possible

identical
exactly the same as something else

idle
not working; not wanting to work

igloo igloos
a house made of snow blocks

ignorant
not wise; knowing little or nothing

ignore
ignores, ignoring, ignored
to deliberately take no notice of someone or something

ill
not well; sick

illness illnesses
what it is that is wrong with you when you are ill; a disease

ill-treat
ill-treats, ill-treating, ill-treated
to treat badly

illustrate
illustrates, illustrating, illustrated
to explain something by drawing pictures; to add pictures to

image images
1 a figure carved in wood or stone; a statue
2 a picture
3 a reflection

imaginary
not real; made up in the mind

imitate
imitates, imitating, imitated
to do the same as somebody else

immediate
1 near; close
2 taking place right away

a
b
c
d
e
f
g
h
i I
j
k
l
m
n
o
p
q
r
s
t
u
v
w
x
y
z

a
b
c
d
e
f
g
h
i I
j
k
l
m
n
o
p
q
r
s
t
u
v
w
x
y
z

immediately

at once

impertinent

rude; having bad manners; cheeky

impolite

rude

import

imports, importing, imported

to bring goods into a country from another country

important

mattering very much

impossible

not able to be done

impress

impresses, impressing, impressed

to make someone notice and admire you

imprison

imprisons, imprisoning, imprisoned

to put into prison

improve

improves, improving, improved

to make something better; to get better

in

when you are inside somewhere; the opposite of out

incapable

not able to do something

inch inches

a small measure of length (about two and a half centimetres); there are 12 inches in a foot

incident incidents

a happening; something that takes place

include

includes, including, included

to put something in with other things

income

money that is earned or received

inconvenient

not suitable or helpful at a particular time

incorrect

wrong

increase

increases, increasing, increased

to make or become larger

indeed

as a matter of fact; really

independent

able to act alone

index indexes

an alphabetical list showing where things can be found in a book

indignant

angry; annoyed

individual individuals

a single person or thing

infant infants

1 a baby; a young child
2 a pupil aged between five and seven years

infectious

when an illness is likely to be passed on to someone else

inflate

inflates, inflating, inflated

to put air into something, causing it to swell

inform

informs, informing, informed

to tell; to give the news

information

facts that you can learn about someone or something

information and communication technology (ICT)

finding, receiving, saving and sending information using a computer; ICT is sometimes a school subject

ingredient ingredients

one of a number of things that together make up something else (in a recipe, for example)

inhabit

inhabits, inhabiting, inhabited

to live in a certain place

initial initials

1 first
2 the first letter of your name
3 the first letter of a word

injection injections

the putting of medicine into the body with a special needle

injure

injures, injuring, injured

to hurt

ink inks

a coloured liquid used for writing or printing

inland

away from the sea

inn inns

a pub or small hotel

innocent

not guilty; not at fault

inquire (sometimes spelt 'enquire')

inquires, inquiring, inquired

to ask questions

insane

not in your right mind; mad

insect insects

a very small creature with six legs

inside

the part that is surrounded by something else

insist

insists, insisting, insisted

to keep on saying something

inspect

inspects, inspecting, inspected

to look carefully at something

instant

1 a moment
2 made in a moment (for example, instant coffee)

instead of

in place of

a
b
c
d
e
f
g
h
i I
j
k
l
m
n
o
p
q
r
s
t
u
v
w
x
y
z

a
b
c
d
e
f
g
h
i I
j
k
l
m
n
o
p
q
r
s
t
u
v
w
x
y
z

instruct
instructs, instructing, instructed

to tell someone what to do or how to do something

instruction instructions
words telling you what to do or how to do something

instrument instruments
1 something on which music is played
2 a tool

insult (say 'in**sult**')
insults, insulting, insulted

to hurt someone's feelings by saying rude or unkind things

intelligent
quick to learn; clever

intend
intends, intending, intended

to mean to do something

interest
keen attention

interesting
worth knowing about

interfere
interferes, interfering, interfered

to get in the way of; to meddle

internet (net)
a way of communicating and finding things out by computer. It makes it possible for you to get in touch with other computers all over the world.

interrupt
interrupts, interrupting, interrupted

to break into what other people are saying or doing

interval intervals
a space between things

interview interviews
a meeting at which people ask and answer questions

introduce
introduces, introducing, introduced

to make people known to each other by name

invade
invades, invading, invaded

to enter, usually using force

invent
invents, inventing, invented

to think of and make something for the first time

inventor inventors
a person who invents things

investigate
investigates, investigating, investigated

to find out about something

invisible
not able to be seen

invitation invitations
when someone asks you to do something (to go to a party, for example)

invite

invites, inviting, invited

to ask somebody to come to your house or to go out with you

irate

very angry

iris

1 the coloured part of your eye
2 a type of plant with long leaves and large flowers

iron irons

1 a tool for smoothing clothes
2 a hard strong metal

irritate

irritates, irritating, irritated

1 to make annoyed or angry
2 to make sore or itchy

island islands

a piece of land with water all round it

isolate

isolates, isolating, isolated

to keep separate from others

itch itches

a tickling of the skin that makes you want to scratch

item items

one thing out of a number of things

ivory

the hard white material that elephants' tusks are made from

ivy

a climbing evergreen plant

jab

jabs, jabbing, jabbed

to poke at or to stab with something pointed

jackal jackals

a wild animal that looks like a dog

jacket jackets

a short coat

jail jails

a prison. The word may also be spelt **gaol**.

jam jams

1 a food made from boiled fruit and sugar
2 something pressed together so that it cannot move any more (the traffic in a traffic jam, for example)

jar jars

a container with a wide opening at the top

jaw jaws

the bone to which teeth are fixed; the lower part of the face

jazz

a kind of music

jealous

annoyed because you wish you had what others have

a b c d e f g h i **j J** k l m n o p q r s t u v w x y z

jeans

trousers made from strong cotton, often blue

jeep jeeps

a small powerful car

jeer

jeers, jeering, jeered

to make rude remarks about something or someone

jelly jellies

a cold clear pudding

jerk jerks

a sudden push or pull

jersey jerseys

a piece of knitted clothing for the upper part of the body; a jumper

jet jets

1 a thin stream of water or air
2 a plane that can fly very fast because it has a special kind of engine

jewel jewels

a valuable stone

jewellery

a decoration that you wear (for example, a necklace, bracelet or ring)

Jewish

to do with the religion called Judaism

jigsaw puzzle (jigsaw) jigsaw puzzles (jigsaws)

a kind of puzzle made of little pieces that you put together to make a picture

jingle

jingles, jingling, jingled

to make a ringing sound with small metal objects

job jobs

1 a piece of work
2 the work someone does to earn money

jockey jockeys

the rider of a race horse

jog

jogs, jogging, jogged

to run for exercise

join

joins, joining, joined

1 to fasten together
2 to start being a member of a group

joiner joiners

a person who works with wood; a carpenter

joint joints

1 the place where two parts fit together
2 a large piece of meat

joke jokes

a funny story, usually quite short

jolly

jollier, jolliest

merry; happy; lively

jolt jolts

a sudden jerk

journey journeys

a trip from place to place

joy

happiness; gladness

joystick joysticks

a control stick for a plane or for computer or video games

jubilant

happy; glad; joyful

judge judges

1 the person who has the final say in a court of law
2 someone who decides the result of a competition
3 to decide what you think after careful thought

judo

a Japanese sport

jug jugs

a container for pouring liquids

juggler jugglers

a person who can keep several objects in the air at the same time without dropping them

juice juices

the liquid that comes from fruit and vegetables

juicy

juicier, juiciest

having a lot of juice

jumble jumbles

a muddle; many things mixed together in an untidy way

jumbo

very big

jump

jumps, jumping, jumped
to spring up and down

jumper jumpers

a knitted piece of clothing worn on the top part of the body

junction junctions

a place where two or more railway lines or roads meet or cross

jungle jungles

a thick forest in a very hot country

junior

1 younger or lower in importance than others
2 a pupil aged between seven and 11 years

junk

1 rubbish that is of no use to anyone
2 a kind of Chinese sailing-boat

junk food

food that is quick to prepare but is not very good for you

just

1 fair; right
2 only

justice

a way of dealing with people that is fair to everyone

justify

justifies, justifying, justified
to explain why something you have done is reasonable

jut

juts, jutting, jutted
to stick out

a
b
c
d
e
f
g
h
i
j J
k
l
m
n
o
p
q
r
s
t
u
v
w
x
y
z

a
b
c
d
e
f
g
h
i
j
k K
l
m
n
o
p
q
r
s
t
u
v
w
x
y
z

kangaroo kangaroos

an Australian animal that jumps using its back legs

karate

a Japanese sport

keel keels

the bottom part of a boat

keen

keener, keenest

liking something very much; wanting to do something, and wanting to do it well

keep

keeps, keeping, kept

to hold; to have for oneself

kennel kennels

a small house for a dog

kerb kerbs

the edge of the pavement

kernel kernels

the centre part of a nut – the part you eat

ketchup

a tomato sauce that is often eaten with burgers or chips

kettle kettles

a container used to boil water

key keys

1 a tool to open or close a lock
2 a part that you press down on a musical instrument or a computer keyboard

keyboard keyboards

1 buttons with letters and numbers on them, which you press when typing on a computer
2 an electric piano

kick

kicks, kicking, kicked

to hit with the foot

kid kids

1 a young goat
2 a child

kidnap

kidnaps, kidnapping, kidnapped

to seize a person and keep him or her until money is paid for their safe return

kidney kidneys

1 one of two small parts inside the body
2 the kidney of an animal used as food

kill

kills, killing, killed

to make someone or something die

kilogram (kilo)

kilograms (kilos)

a measure of mass equal to 1000 grams

kilometre kilometres

a measure of length equal to 1000 metres

kilt kilts

a pleated skirt, usually of tartan cloth, sometimes worn by men in Scotland

kind kinds

1 a type; a sort
2 good; helpful; gentle

king kings

a male head of a country

kingdom kingdoms

an area ruled over by a king or queen

kiosk kiosks

a small hut from which something is sold (for example, tickets or newspapers)

kipper kippers

a herring split open and smoked

kiss

kisses, kissing, kissed

to touch with the lips

kit kits

things you need in order to do something

kitchen kitchens

a room used for cooking

kite kites

a toy that is flown outdoors at the end of a long string

kitten kittens

a young cat

When you see the letters '**kn**' at the beginning of a word, say '**n**'. The '**k**' is silent.

knee knees

the joint in the middle of the leg

kneel

kneels, kneeling, kneeled

to place one or both knees on the ground

knickers

pants that girls and women wear

knife knives

a tool used for cutting

knit

knits, knitting, knitted

to join loops of wool using long needles

knob knobs

a round handle used on doors

knock

knocks, knocking, knocked

1 to make a tapping noise
2 to strike hard

knot knots

a fastening made by twisting and tying string or rope

know

knows, knowing, knew

1 to have something in your mind
2 to have met someone before

knowledge

the facts that you know and understand

k K

a
b
c
d
e
f
g
h
i
j
k K
l
m
n
o
p
q
r
s
t
u
v
w
x
y
z

label labels

paper or a card on which information can be written

labour labours

hard work

lace

1 a pattern made from fine thread
2 a strong string to tie a shoe

lack

lacks, lacking, lacked

to be without something

lad lads

a boy

ladder ladders

a set of steps for getting up to high places

ladle ladles

a large deep spoon with a long handle, used for serving soup

lady ladies

a woman

ladybird ladybirds

a small beetle, often red with black spots

lag

lags, lagging, lagged

to move slowly; to fall behind others

lair lairs

a wild animal's den

lake lakes

a large area of water with land all round it

lamb lambs

a young sheep

lame

not able to walk easily

lamp lamps

something made for giving light

lance lances

a long thin spear

land

1 the part of the earth not covered by the sea
2 to come to land from air or water
3 a country

lane lanes

a narrow road

language languages

the words used by the people of a particular country

lantern lanterns

an old-fashioned lamp with a carrying handle

lap laps

1 the space formed on the top of your thighs when you are sitting down
2 to drink using the tongue, like a dog or cat
3 once round a race track

laptop laptops

a computer that you can carry around with you

larch larches

a kind of tree with cones that loses its leaves in winter

large

larger, largest

big; huge

lark larks

a small singing bird

lasagne

an Italian dish made with pasta, meat and tomato sauce

lash

lashes, lashing, lashed

1 to fasten tightly with rope or string
2 to whip; to hit hard
3 a small hair on the eyelid

lasso (say 'lassoo') lassos

a rope with a noose at the end for catching animals

last

1 coming after all the others
2 to go on for a period of time

late

later, latest

1 coming after the right time
2 near the end of a period of time

lather (say 'larther')

the bubbles made when you use soap and water

laugh laughs

the sound you make when you are amused or happy

launch

launches, launching, launched

1 to put a new boat in the water for the first time
2 to send a rocket into the sky
3 a kind of motor boat

launderette launderettes

a place where you can pay to use washing machines

laundry laundries

1 a place where clothes are washed for you
2 a pile of clothes ready for washing or ironing

lavatory lavatories

a toilet

law laws

a rule made by the government that everyone must obey

lawn lawns

an area of short grass in a garden

lawyer lawyers

a person who has studied the law and can advise people about it

lay

lays, laying, laid

1 to put down carefully
2 to put out knives and forks, ready for a meal
3 to produce eggs

lazy

lazier, laziest

not fond of working; liking to do nothing

lead (sounds like 'bed')

a heavy metal

a
b
c
d
e
f
g
h
i
j
k
l L
m
n
o
p
q
r
s
t
u
v
w
x
y
z

lead (sounds like 'feed')

leads, leading, led

1 to go in front for others to follow
2 a strap or chain fixed to a dog's collar in order to control it

leader leaders

the person in charge of a group

leaf leaves

one of the flat green parts of a plant

league leagues

a group of sports teams who play games against each other to find a winner

leak leaks

liquid, gas or tiny pieces of something that have escaped through a hole or gap

lean

leans, leaning, leant, leaned

1 to bend towards something
2 thin; not fat
3 **lean against** to put your weight against something

leap

leaps, leaping, leapt, leaped

to jump; to spring

learn

learns, learning, learnt, learned

to get to know; to get better at doing something

least

the smallest amount

leather

an animal's skin, specially prepared for making into things

leave

leaves, leaving, left

1 to go away from
2 to let something stay where it is
3 to allow something to stay the same, without changing it

lecture lectures

a speech made to a number of people, usually to teach them something

ledge ledges

a narrow shelf or platform

leek leeks

a long white and green vegetable that tastes rather like an onion

left

the opposite of right

leg legs

1 one of the limbs with which you walk
2 one of the supports at the corner of a chair or table

legal

to do with the law

legend legends

a story from long ago that may not be true

leisure

spare time used for hobbies and enjoying yourself

lemon lemons

a yellow fruit with a sharp taste

lemonade

a sweet drink, usually fizzy

lend

lends, lending, lent

to allow somebody to use something that belongs to you

length lengths

the distance from one end to the other

leopard leopards

a large wild animal of the cat family, with spotted fur

leotard leotards

a close-fitting garment worn for gymnastics or dancing

less

lesser, least

smaller; not so big; not so much

lesson lessons

something to be learned

let

lets, letting, let

1 to allow; to permit
2 to allow someone to use a building in return for money

letter letters

1 a written message sent to somebody by post
2 one of the signs you use for writing (for example, a, b, c)

lettuce lettuces

a vegetable with large green leaves, used in salads

level

1 the same height all along; flat
2 equal

lever levers

a strong metal bar for lifting things

liar liars

a person who tells lies

librarian librarians

a person who works in a library

library libraries

a room or building where books are kept

licence licences

a piece of paper that gives you written permission to do something

lick

licks, licking, licked

to wet something with your tongue; to move your tongue over something

lid lids

a cover that can be opened or taken off

lie

lies, lying, lay

to stretch out flat (on a bed or on the floor, for example)

lie

lies, lying, lied

1 to say things that are not true
2 something that is not true

life lives

the time when you are alive

lifeboat lifeboats

a special boat used to rescue sailors and others who are in danger at sea

a
b
c
d
e
f
g
h
i
j
k
l L
m
n
o
p
q
r
s
t
u
v
w
x
y
z

a b c d e f g h i j k l L m n o p q r s t u v w x y z

lift
lifts, lifting, lifted

1 to raise
2 a machine that carries people or things up or down between the floors in a building
3 a ride in someone else's vehicle

light

1 brightness that comes from the sun and from lamps and candles
2 pale in colour; not dark
3 having little weight; easy to lift
4 to set on fire

lighthouse lighthouses

a tower with a bright light on top to warn ships of danger

lightning

a flash of light you see in the sky during a thunderstorm

like
likes, liking, liked

1 to be fond of
2 the same as; similar to

likely
likelier, likeliest

as you would expect

lilac lilacs

1 a small tree with sweet-smelling purple or white flowers
2 a pale purple colour

lily lilies

a beautiful flower, often white, pink or yellow in colour

limb limbs

an arm, a leg or a wing

lime limes

1 a green fruit like a small lemon
2 a kind of tree with large pale-green leaves
3 a white powder made from limestone

limestone

a greyish-white rock

limit limits

the end; as far as you can go

limp
limps, limping, limped

1 the way you walk if you have hurt your foot or your leg
2 not firm or stiff

line lines

1 a long thin mark
2 people or things standing one behind the other; a queue

linen

a kind of thin cloth

liner liners

a large passenger ship

lining linings

a material used on the inside of something (clothes or curtains, for example)

link links

one of the rings in a chain

lion lions

a large wild animal of the cat family

lip lips

one of the outer edges of the mouth

lipstick lipsticks

colouring for the lips

liquid liquids

something that flows (for example, water or milk)

liquorice (say 'lickerish')

a kind of chewy black sweet made from a plant root

list lists

a number of names or things written down one after the other

listen

listens, listening, listened

1 to try to hear
2 to take notice of what someone is saying

literacy

being able to read and write

literature

well-written stories and poems

litre litres

a measure of liquid (equal to 1000 millilitres)

litter

1 rubbish lying about
2 a number of animals born together

little

small

live

lives, living, lived

1 to stay in a place
2 to be alive

lively

livelier, liveliest

full of life; active

liver livers

1 a part of the inside of the body
2 the liver of an animal used as food

lizard lizards

an animal with four short legs, a long tail and skin like a snake's

load

loads, loading, loaded

1 to put things on to a vehicle or a ship
2 as much as can be carried at one time

loaf loaves

a large piece of bread that may be cut into slices

loan loans

something that is lent or borrowed

lobster lobsters

a kind of large shellfish with claws

local

near a particular place; near where you are

loch (say 'lock') lochs

a Scottish lake

lock

locks, locking, locked

1 to fasten something so that only a key will open it
2 a place in a canal or river where boats are raised or lowered
3 a piece of hair

a
b
c
d
e
f
g
h
i
j
k
l L
m
n
o
p
q
r
s
t
u
v
w
x
y
z

a
b
c
d
e
f
g
h
i
j
k
l L
m
n
o
p
q
r
s
t
u
v
w
x
y
z

locust locusts

an insect like a grasshopper that destroys crops

loft lofts

a room just under the roof of a house

log logs

1 a large piece of wood sawn off a tree
2 a formal diary of what happens each day (on a ship, for example)

lollipop (lolly)

lollipops (lollies)

a sweet on the end of a stick (see also **ice lolly**)

lonely

lonelier, loneliest

feeling sad and alone; without friends

long

longer, longest

1 of great length; not short
2 to wish for something very much

look

looks, looking, looked

1 to try to see
2 to appear to be; to seem
3 **look after** to care for; to make sure that another living thing has all that it needs

loop loops

a long thin circle made with a piece of thread, such as cotton, wool or string

loose

looser, loosest

not tied or fixed; free to move

lord lords

a title given to a man by a king or queen

lorry lorries

a large vehicle for carrying heavy things

lose

loses, losing, lost

1 not to be able to find something
2 to be beaten; not to win

loss losses

something you have lost

lost

missing; not findable; unable to find your way

loud

louder, loudest

making a lot of noise

lounge lounges

1 a sitting room
2 to act lazily

louse lice

a small insect that can live in your hair

love

loves, loving, loved

to like very much

lovely

lovelier, loveliest

beautiful

low
lower, lowest

1 not high; near to the ground; close to the bottom of something
2 quiet; not loud

luck
fortune; chance

lucky
luckier, luckiest
having good luck

luggage
bags and suitcases you take with you when travelling

lukewarm
neither warm nor cold

lullaby lullabies
a quiet song to send a baby to sleep

lump lumps
1 a swelling
2 a piece of something

lunch lunches
a meal eaten in the middle of day

lung lungs
part of the body with which you breathe (you have two lungs)

luxury luxuries
something expensive you like having but do not need

lying
saying things that are not true; telling lies

machine machines
something made out of many parts that work together to do a job

machinery
machines; parts of a machine

mackerel mackerel
a kind of sea fish used as food

mad
madder, maddest
1 crazy; very foolish
2 very angry

Madam
a polite way of speaking or writing to a woman

magazine magazines
a thin book with things to read and many photos; it comes out once a week or once a month

maggot maggots
a grub that turns into a fly (sometimes found in old meat, for example)

magic
strange and wonderful things that happen

magician magicians
a person who performs magic tricks or makes wonderful things happen

a b c d e f g h i j k l **m M** n o p q r s t u v w x y z

a
b
c
d
e
f
g
h
i
j
k
l
m M
n
o
p
q
r
s
t
u
v
w
x
y
z

magnet magnets

a piece of iron or steel that attracts other pieces of iron or steel

magnificent

splendid

magnify

magnifies, magnifying, magnified

to make something appear larger

magpie magpies

a black and white bird with a long tail

maid maids

1 a woman servant
2 an old word for a girl

mail

letters and parcels sent by post

main

most important

maize

a kind of grain used for food; sweetcorn

Majesty Majesties

a title given to a king or queen

major majors

1 an officer in the army
2 important or large

make

makes, making, made

1 to build; to put things together to make something new
2 to force somebody to do something

male males

a person or an animal that can one day be a father; a man or boy

mammal mammals

an animal that feeds its young with its own milk

mammoth mammoths

1 a kind of large elephant from long ago
2 very big; huge

man men

a grown-up male person

manage

manages, managing, managed

to be able to do something

manager managers

a person in charge of something

mane manes

the long hair on the neck of an animal, especially a horse or lion

manger mangers

an animal's feeding-box in a stable

mango mangoes or mangos

a large, sweet yellowish fruit

manner manners

1 the way you behave
2 the way something is done

manners

behaviour, especially good behaviour towards other people

mansion mansions

a very large house

manufacture

manufactures, manufacturing, manufactured

to make things in a factory by using machinery

many

more, most

a lot of; plenty

map maps

a drawing or plan that helps you find your way around a place

maple maples

a kind of tree that produces a thick sticky liquid

marble marbles

1 a small glass or stone ball, used as a toy
2 a type of hard stone that can be polished smooth

march

marches, marching, marched

to walk with others, sometimes to music

mare mares

a female horse

margarine

a food made from vegetable oils, often used instead of butter

margin margins

a border down the side of a page

mark marks

1 a sign put on something
2 a spot; a stain
3 to put a mark on
4 the score you are given for work you have done (in a test, for example)

market markets

a place where goods are bought and sold

marmalade

a kind of jam, usually made of oranges or lemons

maroon

1 a very dark red colour
2 to be left in a place you cannot get away from (for example, on an island)

marriage marriages

1 the life that two married people share
2 a wedding

marry

marries, marrying, married

to start being someone's husband or wife

marsh marshes

wet land; a swamp; a bog

marvellous

wonderful

marzipan

a paste made from almonds, egg and sugar, put on cakes

mascot mascots

a charm; a thing, animal or person that is supposed to bring good luck

masculine

to do with men or boys

mash

mashes, mashing, mashed

to crush something until it is soft and smooth (for example, potatoes)

a b c d e f g h i j k l m **M** n o p q r s t u v w x y z

a
b
c
d
e
f
g
h
i
j
k
l
m M
n
o
p
q
r
s
t
u
v
w
x
y
z

mask masks

a covering for the face

mass

1 how heavy something is
2 a large amount or number of things
3 a religious ceremony, especially in a Roman Catholic church

massive

very large; enormous

mast masts

the tall pole used to hold up the sails on a ship

mat mats

a small rug

match matches

1 a small stick with a tip that catches fire easily
2 a game between two teams
3 to be the same as something else

mate mates

companion; friend

material materials

1 anything from which things can be made
2 cloth

mathematics (maths)

the study of numbers, shapes and measurements

matter matters

1 something you think about
2 to be important

mattress mattresses

a large thick layer of material on which you sleep

maybe

perhaps; possibly

mayor mayors

the chief person in a town

maze mazes

paths or lines arranged so that it is difficult to find your way through them

meadow meadows

an area of wild grass

meal meals

the food you eat at a certain time of day (for example, lunch)

mean
meaner, meanest

1 selfish
2 **mean to** to have it in your mind to

meaning meanings

what you have in your mind when you say or write something; an explanation

measles

an illness that gives you red spots

measure
measures, measuring, measured

1 to find out how long or heavy something is
2 a unit for measuring

measurement measurements

what something measures

meat

flesh from an animal used as food

mechanic mechanics (say 'meckanic')

a person who makes or repairs machinery

medal medals

a metal disc given as a reward for something you have done

meddle

meddles, meddling, meddled

to interfere with things that are not your business

medicine medicines

something you take to make you better when you are ill; a drug

medium

not big or small; in between

meek

meeker, meekest

gentle

meet

meets, meeting, met

1 to come together
2 to be in the same place as someone so that you can talk

melody melodies

a tune

melon melons

a large juicy fruit with a green or yellow skin

melt

melts, melting, melted

to turn into liquid because of heat

member members

a person who belongs to a group

memory memories

1 the part of the brain with which you remember
2 a thought about the past

mend

mends, mending, mended

to put right; to repair

mental

to do with the mind

mention

mentions, mentioning, mentioned

to talk about briefly

menu menus

a list of things you can eat in a restaurant

merchant merchants

a person who buys and sells

mercy mercies

pity; not punishing someone

merry

merrier, merriest

happy; cheerful; joyful

mess messes

things mixed together in an untidy way

message messages

information or instructions sent from one person to another

metal metals

materials such as iron, steel, gold, silver and brass

a b c d e f g h i j k l

m M

n o p q r s t u v w x y z

meteor meteors

a small object from space that travels very fast and burns up when it enters the earth's atmosphere

meter meters

a machine for measuring things (gas, electricity or water, for example)

method methods

the way something is done

metre (say 'meeter') metres

a measure of length equal to 100 centimetres

microphone (mike) microphones (mikes)

a piece of equipment that records your voice or makes it sound louder

microscope microscopes

an instrument used to make very small things look much bigger

microwave microwaves

a special kind of electronic oven that cooks food quickly

midday

12 o'clock in the day; noon

middle middles

the part of something that is the same distance from each end or side

midnight

12 o'clock at night

mild

milder, mildest

1 gentle; not rough
2 not hot or too cold

mile miles

a measure of distance

milk

a white liquid produced by mothers and some female animals to feed their babies

milkshake milkshakes

a drink made from milk, sometimes with a special taste (for example, strawberry or chocolate)

mill mills

1 a place where grain is ground into flour
2 a kind of factory
3 a small machine for making things into a fine powder

millennium millennia

1000 years

millimetre millimetres

a measure of length; there are 1000 millimetres in a metre

million millions

1 000 000; a number

millionaire millionaires

a rich person who has at least a million pounds

mime

mimes, miming, mimed

to use actions instead of words to show the meaning of something

mimic

mimics, mimicking, mimicked

to speak or act like someone else

mince

minces, mincing, minced

to chop up very small

mind

minds, minding, minded

1 to look after
2 a person's way of thinking; the
   power to think

mine

1 belonging to me
2 a place where minerals are dug
   from the earth (for example,
   coal)

mineral minerals

a material such as rock that is dug
out of the earth

mingle

mingles, mingling, mingled

to mix

miniature

very small (a copy of something
bigger)

minibus minibuses

a small bus with lots of seats for
carrying people

minister ministers

1 a person in charge of
   a church
2 an important member of a
   government

minor

smaller or less important

mint mints

1 a plant used to flavour food
2 a sweet flavoured with mint
3 a place where coins are made

minus

less; without; the sign −

minute (say 'minit') minutes

a length of time of 60 seconds;
there are 60 minutes in one hour

minute (say 'my**newt**')

very small

miracle miracles

a strange and wonderful happening

mirror mirrors

a piece of glass in which you can
see yourself

mischief

stupid actions that cause trouble

mischievous

naughty; always doing mischief

miser misers

a person who has plenty of money
but tries not to spend any

miserable

full of sadness

misery miseries

great unhappiness; sorrow

miss

misses, missing, missed

not to see or find

Miss

a title given to a woman or girl
who is not married

missing

lost; not findable; left out

mission missions

an important task that someone is sent to do

missionary missionaries

a person who is sent to other places to teach people about religion

mist

drops of water in the air that stop you seeing properly; fog

mistake mistakes

something you have done that is wrong

mistletoe

an evergreen plant with white berries

mitten mittens

a glove with only two parts, one for the fingers and one for the thumb

mix

mixes, mixing, mixed

to put things together

mixture mixtures

things mixed together

moan moans

a low sound made when you are in pain or unhappy

moat moats

a ditch round a castle to keep it safe from attack

mobile

1 able to move
2 a decoration with hanging parts that move in the breeze

mobile phone (mobile)

mobile phones (mobiles)

a phone that you can use almost anywhere

mock

mocks, mocking, mocked

to make fun of someone

model models

1 a small copy of something
2 a pattern to be followed
3 a person who wears clothes to show them to people

modern

up-to-date; belonging to the present time

moist

a little wet; damp

mole moles

1 a small furry animal that burrows underground
2 a small dark spot on the skin

moment moments

a very short space of time

monarch monarchs

a ruler who is a king or queen

monastery monasteries

a place where monks live

money

the coins and notes that you use when buying and selling things

mongrel mongrels

a dog of two or more breeds

monk monks

a man who has given his life to his religion and who lives in a monastery

monkey monkeys

an animal with a long tail; it has hands and feet a bit like ours

monster monsters

a large frightening creature that you read about in stories

month months

1 one of the 12 parts of the year
2 a period of four weeks

monument monuments

something built in memory of an important person or event

mood moods

the way you feel

moon

the round object that goes around the earth and can be seen in the sky at night

moor moors

1 a large area of rough ground, covered with grass and heather
2 to fasten a boat with a rope

mop mops

soft material at the end of a long pole, used for cleaning

moral morals

a lesson about right and wrong (for example, one that you learn from a story)

more

a greater number or amount

morning mornings

the part of the day before noon

mosque mosques

a place where Muslims worship

mosquito mosquitoes

a small flying insect that bites and can spread disease

moss mosses

a furry green plant that grows on wet ground, stones and trees

most

the greatest number or amount

moth moths

an insect like a butterfly that usually flies at night

mother mothers

a female parent

motion motions

movement

motor motors

a machine that makes things move

motorway motorways

a wide road where vehicles can go fast

mould

moulds, moulding, moulded

1 to make something into a new shape
2 a container for shaping things

mound mounds

a large heap; a small hill

a b c d e f g h i j k l **m M** n o p q r s t u v w x y z

a
b
c
d
e
f
g
h
i
j
k
l
m M
n
o
p
q
r
s
t
u
v
w
x
y
z

mount

mounts, mounting, mounted

to get onto (a horse or a bicycle, for example)

mountain mountains

a very large and steep hill

mourn

mourns, mourning, mourned

to be very sad because someone has died or because you have lost something

mouse mice

1 a small animal with a long tail
2 a small piece of equipment that you use to move the pointer on a computer

moustache moustaches

hair growing on the top lip

mouth mouths

1 the part of the face with which you speak, eat and drink
2 where a river goes into the sea

move

moves, moving, moved

to go or take from one place to another

movement movements

what happens when someone or something moves

movie movies

a film; a story shown in a cinema

mow

mows, mowing, mowed

to cut grass

Mr (say 'mister')

title given to a man

Mrs (say 'missiz')

title given to a married woman

Ms (say 'miz')

title given to a woman who may or may not be married

much

a large quantity

mud

wet earth

muddle muddles

a mixed-up state

mug mugs

a big cup, usually with straight sides

multiply

multiplies, multiplying, multiplied

to add the same number many times (×)

Mummy (Mum) mummies (mums)

1 a name for your mother
2 **mummy** a dead body that has been preserved

mumps

a painful illness that gives you a sore neck and throat

munch

munches, munching, munched

to eat noisily

murmur

murmurs, murmuring, murmured

to speak very quietly

muscle muscles

one of the parts of the body that you use to move

museum museums

a building where old and interesting things can be seen

mushroom mushrooms

a kind of plant that is shaped like a small umbrella. Some mushrooms can be eaten but others are poisonous.

music

pleasant sounds made by people singing or playing instruments or by special electronic equipment

musical

1 to do with music
2 a special type of film or a play using music

Muslim Muslims

a follower of a particular religion whose holy book is the Qur'an

mustard

a hot-tasting yellow powder or paste used to flavour food

mutter

mutters, muttering, muttered

to speak or complain in a quiet voice

mysterious

very strange

mystery mysteries

something strange that cannot be explained

nag

nags, nagging, nagged

to keep finding fault with someone

nail nails

1 the hard shiny covering at the end of a finger or toe
2 a small pointed piece of metal used to join pieces of wood together

naked

not wearing any clothes; not covered; bare

name names

what you call someone or something

napkin napkins

a piece of cloth or paper that keeps your clothes clean while you eat

nappy nappies

a paper pad or a piece of cloth for wrapping round a baby's bottom

narrow

narrower, narrowest

not far across; not wide

nasty

nastier, nastiest

not pleasant; not good to taste

nation nations

the people of one country

a
b
c
d
e
f
g
h
i
j
k
l
m
n N
o
p
q
r
s
t
u
v
w
x
y
z

a b c d e f g h i j k l m **n N** o p q r s t u v w x y z

national

belonging to a nation

native natives

a person born in a certain place

natural

made by nature; not made by people

nature

1 everything in the world not made by people (for example, the weather, animals, plants and rocks)
2 the way people or other living things behave

naughty

naughtier, naughtiest

badly behaved

naval

to do with a navy

navel navels

your tummy button

navigate

navigates, navigating, navigated

to decide which way a vehicle should go when on a journey

navy navies

1 the sailors whose job it is to protect their country
2 a dark blue colour

near

nearer, nearest

close to

nearby

close

nearly

almost

neat

neater, neatest

tidy; done carefully

necessary

needed; needing to be done

neck necks

the part of the body joining the head and the shoulders

necklace necklaces

a string of beads or jewels worn round the neck

need

needs, needing, needed

to have to have something; to have to do something; to want

needle needles

a tiny stick of metal with a sharp point at one end and a hole at the other end, used for sewing

neglect

neglects, neglecting, neglected

not to do something that should be done; not to look after properly

neigh

the sound a horse makes

neighbour neighbours

a person who lives next door or quite near

nephew nephews

a son of a brother or sister

nerve nerves

one of the small parts of the body that carry messages to and from the brain

nervous

afraid; easily frightened or worried

nest nests

a place used as a home by birds and some animals

net nets

1 threads of string or wire twisted together. It lets small objects through but catches larger ones.
2 see **internet**

netball

a team game in which a ball is thrown into a high net

nettle nettles

a wild plant that stings when touched

new

newer, newest

just made or bought; not used or known before

news

information about something that has just happened

newspaper (paper)
newspapers (papers)

sheets of paper printed every day or every week to give news

newt newts

a land or water animal like a small lizard

next

1 nearest
2 following

nibble

nibbles, nibbling, nibbled

to eat in tiny bites

nice

nicer, nicest

pleasant

nickname nicknames

a name that is not your real name

niece nieces

a daughter of a brother or sister

night nights

the time of day when it is dark

nightdress (nightie)
nightdresses (nighties)

a loose kind of dress worn in bed by girls and women

nightmare nightmares

a bad or frightening dream

nimble

nimbler, nimblest

quick and light on your feet

nine

9; a number

nineteen

19; a number

ninety

90; a number

nip

nips, nipping, nipped

to bite; to pinch

a
b
c
d
e
f
g
h
i
j
k
l
m
n N
o
p
q
r
s
t
u
v
w
x
y
z

a
b
c
d
e
f
g
h
i
j
k
l
m
n N
o
p
q
r
s
t
u
v
w
x
y
z

noble

nobler, noblest

1 of very good character
2 of high rank

nod

nods, nodding, nodded

to bend your head forward quickly, often as a sign that you mean 'yes'

noise noises

a sound, often loud and unpleasant

none

not any; not one

non-fiction

a piece of writing that tells you about real things (for example, real people, real places or things that have really happened)

nonsense

words that do not make sense

noodles

very long thin strips of pasta, often used in Chinese cooking

noon

12 o'clock in the day; midday

noose nooses

a loop in a rope that can be made tighter by pulling

normal

usual; the same as others

north

the direction that is on the left as you face the rising sun

nose noses

the part of your face that you use to breathe and to smell things through

nostril nostrils

one of the two openings in your nose

notch notches

a small v-shaped cut

note notes

1 a short letter
2 a single sound in music
3 a piece of paper money; a bank note

notice

notices, noticing, noticed

1 to see something
2 a piece of paper stuck to a wall; a sign that tells you something

noun nouns

a word that tells you what a person or thing is called

now

at this moment

nozzle nozzles

the open end of a tube or spout

nude

not wearing any clothes

nudge nudges

a slight push

nugget nuggets

a rough lump, especially of something valuable (gold, for example)

nuisance nuisances

something that annoys you or makes things difficult for you

numb (say 'num')

number, numbest

not having any feeling

number numbers

a word or figure that tells you how many (for example, one, two, three, 1, 2, 3)

numeracy

being able to work with numbers

numerous

many

nun nuns

a woman who has given her life to religion and lives in a convent

nurse nurses

a person trained to care for the sick and to help you keep well

nursery nurseries

1 a place where young children are looked after and can play and learn
2 a place where young plants are grown

nut nuts

1 the hard seed of a tree
2 a piece of metal with a hole in the middle

nutmeg

a spice used in cooking

nylon

cloth made from artificial threads

oak oaks

a large tree with fruits called acorns

oar oars

a pole with a flat end, used to move a boat through water

oasis oases

a place in the desert where water can be found and some plants grow

oats

plants that produce grain used for food (for example, porridge)

obedience

when you obey

obey

obeys, obeying, obeyed

to do as you are told

object (say 'object') objects

1 something that you can see or touch
2 in a sentence, the thing that is having something done to it

object (say 'object')

objects, objecting, objected

to say that you do not like or do not agree to something

oblige

obliges, obliging, obliged

1 to do someone a favour
2 to force someone to do something

a b c d e f g h i j k l m n o **O** p q r s t u v w x y z

a
b
c
d
e
f
g
h
i
j
k
l
m
n
o O
p
q
r
s
t
u
v
w
x
y
z

oblong oblongs

a rectangle; a shape like a square but with two sides longer than the other two, like this page

observe

observes, observing, observed

to see; to look at; to notice

obstacle obstacles

something that is in the way

obstinate

not willing to change your mind or give way to others

obstruct

obstructs, obstructing, obstructed

to block the way; to hold back

obtain

obtains, obtaining, obtained

to get

obvious

easy to see or understand

occasion occasions

a time when something happens

occasionally

sometimes; not very often

occupation occupations

your job; what you work at; something you do

occupy

occupies, occupying, occupied

1 to live in
2 to take up space or time

occur

occurs, occurring, occurred

1 to take place; to happen
2 to come into your mind

ocean oceans

a very large sea

o'clock

the hour shown by the clock

octagon octagons

a flat shape that has eight sides

octopus octopuses

a sea creature with eight long arms

odd

1 not even (for example, 1, 3 and 5 are odd numbers)
2 strange

off

1 when something is not working; the opposite of **on**
2 when food has gone bad

offend

offends, offending, offended

to hurt someone's feelings

offer

offers, offering, offered

1 to hold something out for someone to take
2 to say that you are ready to do something or give something to another person

office offices

a place where people work, usually at desks

officer officers

1 a person who is in charge of other people (for example, in the army) and makes decisions
2 a person with an important position in an organisation

official

something given or said by people in power

often

many times

ogre ogres

in stories, a giant who eats people; a cruel person

oil oils

a smooth and greasy liquid

ointment ointments

a healing cream to put on cuts and bruises

old

older, oldest

1 bought, made or born a long time ago; not new or young
2 having lived for a certain number of years
3 **old fashioned** like something from a long time ago

omelette omelettes

eggs beaten together and fried

on

1 when something is working; the opposite of **off**
2 when something is placed on top of something else

once

1 one time
2 in the past

one

1 1; a number
2 a single person or thing

onion onions

a round vegetable with a very strong smell and taste

online

on the internet

only

1 by itself; alone
2 not more than

onward (or onwards)

on and on; forward

ooze

oozes, oozing, oozed

to flow slowly

open

not shut; not covered over

open air

outdoor

operate

operates, operating, operated

1 to work (a machine, for example)
2 to cut the body open to mend it and make it healthy again

operation operations

when doctors cut open a person's body to repair or remove something

opinion opinions

what you think about something

opponent opponents

someone who disagrees with you or fights against you

opportunity opportunities

the chance or the time to do something

a
b
c
d
e
f
g
h
i
j
k
l
m
n
o O
p
q
r
s
t
u
v
w
x
y
z

a
b
c
d
e
f
g
h
i
j
k
l
m
n
o **O**
p
q
r
s
t
u
v
w
x
y
z

opposite opposites

1 the side facing you
2 as different as possible

optician opticians

a person who fits you with glasses or contact lenses to improve your eyesight

orange oranges

1 a round and juicy fruit that is grown in some hot countries
2 the colour of this fruit

orbit orbits

the path of one body round another in space

orchard orchards

a place where fruit trees are grown

orchestra orchestras

a large group of people playing different musical instruments together

ordeal ordeals

a time when you suffer a lot of pain, fear or worry

order
orders, ordering, ordered

1 to say what must be done or what things you want to buy
2 neatly arranged things or ideas

ordinary

usual; what you expect

ore

rock in which metal is found

organ organs

1 a large musical instrument with many pipes, played like a piano
2 a part of the inside of the body that does something special

organisation organisations

a large group of people who work together; a business; a company

origin origins

the beginning of something

original

the earliest; the first one

ornament ornaments

something used for decoration, especially in a room

orphan orphans

a child whose father and mother have both died

ostrich ostriches

a very large African bird that cannot fly

other

not the same; different

otter otters

a fish-eating animal that lives near water

out

1 not inside
2 away from home
3 not lit; not burning

outdoors

in the open air; not in a building

outfit outfits

a complete set of clothes or equipment

outing outings

a journey made for pleasure; a trip

outlaw outlaws

a person from long ago who broke the law again and again

outline outlines

1 the outside edge of a shape
2 the main facts about something

outside

not inside; not in a building or room

outskirts

the parts of a town that are not in the centre

outstanding

very good

outwards

moving away from the centre of something

oval

egg-shaped

oven ovens

a cooker that you can put things inside for baking

over

1 above
2 finished
3 more than
4 across

overall overalls

a special piece of clothing for working in, worn over your ordinary clothes

overboard

over the side of a ship

overdue

late

overhead

above you; in the sky

overlook

overlooks, overlooking, overlooked

1 to take no notice of
2 to look down on

overtake

overtakes, overtaking, overtook

to catch up with and then pass

owe

owes, owing, owed

to be in debt; to have to pay

owl owls

a bird with large eyes that hunts at night

own

owns, owning, owned

1 to have
2 belonging to yourself

ox oxen

a kind of bull that is usually kept to pull heavy loads and ploughs

oxygen

a gas without taste, smell or colour that is an important part of air and water. You need it to stay alive.

oyster oysters

a kind of shellfish

a b c d e f g h i j k l m n o **O** p q r s t u v w x y z

pP

pace paces
1 a step; a stride
2 the speed at which you walk, run or move

pack
packs, packing, packed
1 to put things into a box, parcel or suitcase
2 a group of things (animals or playing cards, for example); things that are packed together

packet packets
a small box or container made of paper or cardboard

pad pads
1 several sheets of paper stuck together at the top edge
2 something soft and thick that is used to clean or protect things

paddle
paddles, paddling, paddled
1 to walk and splash around in shallow water for fun
2 a long piece of wood with a wide flat end, used to move a canoe or small boat

padlock padlocks
a small lock on a ring that is not fixed to the thing it is locking

page pages
one side of a piece of paper in a book, newspaper or magazine

pageant pageants
a colourful parade or display of scenes from history

pain pains
the unpleasant feeling you get when you are hurt or when you are ill

paint
paints, painting, painted
1 to put paint on something; to make a picture
2 a coloured liquid used to cover something

painting paintings
a picture that is painted

pair pairs
two things of the same kind; a set of two

palace palaces
a large building lived in by an important person (for example, a king or a queen)

pale
paler, palest
with little colour

palm palms
1 a kind of tree that grows in hot countries
2 the flat inside part of the hand

pamper
pampers, pampering, pampered
to give someone more kindness and comfort than they really need

pan pans
a round metal pot with a long handle, used for cooking

pancake pancakes

a thin cake of flour, eggs, milk and sometimes sugar, fried in a pan

panda pandas

a black and white animal like a small bear

pane panes

one of the pieces of glass that make a window

panel panels

a piece of wood or other material fitted into a frame or into a door

panic

sudden alarm or fear that makes it difficult for a person to be sensible

pant

pants, panting, panted

to breathe quickly with an open mouth, especially after running

panther panthers

a large, black wild animal of the cat family

pantomime pantomimes

a fairy story performed on the stage with music and songs

pants

see **underpants**

paper

1 material for writing, printing, drawing or painting on
2 a newspaper

parable parables

a story with a special meaning that teaches you something

parachute parachutes

a huge cloth shaped like an umbrella, attached with strings to a person's back. If a person wearing a parachute jumps out of an aircraft, he or she floats down gently instead of falling.

parade

parades, parading, paraded

1 to march up and down
2 a marching display by people in uniform or costume

paradise

a place of complete happiness

paragraph paragraphs

a group of sentences, the first of which starts on a new line

parallel

the same distance apart all the way along

paralysed

unable to move some or all of the body (for example, because of serious injury)

parcel parcels

something wrapped up for posting or carrying

pardon

forgiveness for something you have done wrong

parent parents

a father or mother

parish parishes

a district looked after by a church minister

a
b
c
d
e
f
g
h
i
j
k
l
m
n
o
p P
q
r
s
t
u
v
w
x
y
z

park parks
1 a piece of land where you can go to play, walk or enjoy yourself. It usually has grass and flowers.
2 to leave a vehicle somewhere for a time

parliament parliaments
1 a group of people who make the laws of a country
2 the place where they meet

parrot parrots
a bird that has brightly-coloured feathers and a curved beak

parsley
a herb used in cooking

parsnip parsnips
a pale root vegetable

part parts
one piece of a whole thing

particular
1 special; different from others
2 hard to please

partner partners
one of two people who do something together (for example, play a game, work together, live together, dance together)

party parties
a group of people gathered together to enjoy themselves and have fun

pass
passes, passing, passed
1 to leave behind; to go past
2 to get through a test

passage passages
1 a narrow way through
2 a piece taken from a book or story

passenger passengers
someone who is travelling in a vehicle but is not driving it

passport passports
a special book containing important information about you, including your name and photograph. You need it when you travel to most other countries.

past
1 the time that has gone before
2 up to and away from

pasta
an Italian food, made with flour, eggs and water, that comes in many different shapes

paste pastes
a wet and sticky mixture that can be spread easily

pastime pastimes
a hobby; interesting work done in your spare time

pastry
a mixture of flour, water and fat, used for baking pies and tarts

pat
pats, patting, patted
to touch gently with the hand

patch patches
a small piece of material used to repair a hole

path paths

a narrow track for walking

patient

1 able to wait calmly
2 someone who is ill and seeing a doctor or dentist
3 someone who is staying in hospital

patrol patrols

a small group of police officers or soldiers

patter

the sound made by drops of rain or running feet

pattern patterns

1 lines and shapes repeated in a way that looks good
2 a plan to follow when making something

pause pauses

a short stop or wait

pavement pavements

the path that you walk on beside a street

paw paws

a foot of an animal such as a dog or cat

pay

pays, paying, paid

1 to hand over money for something
2 money you are given for working

PC

short for **personal computer**

pea peas

a round green seed that grows in a pod, used as food

peace

1 quietness; stillness; calm
2 not being at war

peach peaches

a round juicy fruit with a soft furry skin and a large hard seed inside

peacock peacocks

a large male bird with a beautiful tail shaped like a fan; the female is called a peahen

peak peaks

1 the top of a hill or a mountain
2 the part of a cap that is at the front and sticks out

peal peals

1 the sound made by large bells ringing
2 the sound of thunder or laughter

peanut peanuts

a small round seed like a nut, used as food

pear pears

a soft and juicy yellow or green fruit, with a rounded shape that gets narrow at the top

pearl pearls

a precious gem found in some oyster shells

pebble pebbles

a small smooth stone, sometimes found on the beach

a
b
c
d
e
f
g
h
i
j
k
l
m
n
o
p P
q
r
s
t
u
v
w
x
y
z

peck

pecks, pecking, pecked

to pick up food with the beak;
to poke at

peculiar

strange; unusual

pedal pedals

the part of a bike that you push
on with your feet

pedestrian pedestrians

a person who walks

peel

1 the outside skin of fruit or
  vegetables
2 to take off the outer covering

peep

peeps, peeping, peeped

to look at quickly and secretly; to
glance

peer

peers, peering, peered

1 to look at closely
2 a person of high rank

peg pegs

1 a curved piece of metal or
  plastic on which you hang
  things (your coat, for example)
2 a little piece of wood or plastic
  with a spring inside, for fixing
  clothes to a washing-line

pelican pelicans

a large bird that stores food in a
pouch under its beak

pen pens

1 a writing tool containing ink
2 a place fenced in to keep
  animals together

penalty penalties

a punishment for breaking a rule
or the law

pence (see penny)

plural of penny

pencil pencils

a writing tool made of wood with
a coloured or grey centre

penguin penguins

a large black and white sea bird
that lives in very cold places. It
cannot fly but it can swim.

penknife penknives

a small knife with a folding blade

penny pennies **or** pence

a small British coin; there are
100 pence in a pound

pentagon pentagons

a flat shape that has five sides

people

men, women and children

pepper

1 a white or black powder, often
  used with salt to flavour food
2 a hollow vegetable that can be
  red, yellow or green

peppermint

a flavouring used in sweets and
toothpastes

perch

perches, perching, perched

1 to sit on the edge of something
2 a bar on which a bird can rest

perfect

without fault; complete

perform
performs, performing, performed

to do something, sometimes in front of an audience

performance performances

something done in front of an audience

perfume perfumes

scent; a pleasant smell

perhaps

maybe; possibly

period periods

a length of time

permanent

not coming to an end; lasting for all time, for ever

permission

being allowed to do something

permit
permits, permitting, permitted

to allow; to let someone do something

persist
persists, persisting, persisted

to do something again and again; to refuse to stop

person people

a man, a woman or a child

personal

belonging to a particular person

personal computer (PC)
personal computers (PCs)

a computer that is used by one or two people at a time

perspire
perspires, perspiring, perspired

to sweat

persuade
persuades, persuading, persuaded

to give someone reasons for believing or doing something until the person agrees

pest pests

a person, an animal or an insect that annoys you or causes damage

pester
pesters, pestering, pestered

to keep annoying somebody

pet pets

an animal that you look after at home

petal petals

one of the parts of a flower, often brightly coloured to attract insects

petition petitions

a letter or form, usually signed by a lot of people asking for something

petrol

the liquid that drives the engine of a vehicle

pew pews

a seat or bench in a church

a b c d e f g h i j k l m n o p P q r s t u v w x y z

a b c d e f g h i j k l m n o **p P** q r s t u v w x y z

pheasant pheasant, pheasants

a large colourful bird with a long tail

phone phones

a telephone

photocopier photocopiers

a machine for making a photocopy

photocopy

photocopies, photocopying, photocopied

1 to produce an exact copy of something using a photocopier

2 an exact copy made using a photocopier

photograph (photo) photographs (photos)

a picture taken using a camera

phrase phrases

a few words that are part of a sentence

physical

belonging to the natural world or the body

physics

the science of energy and forces; physics is sometimes a school subject

pianist pianists

a person who plays the piano

piano pianos

a large musical instrument with black and white keys

pick

picks, picking, picked

1 to gather

2 to choose

3 a pointed metal tool with a wooden handle for making holes in hard ground

pickle pickles

vegetables kept in vinegar or salty water

picnic picnics

a meal eaten in the open air

picture pictures

a drawing, a painting or a photograph of something

pie pies

fruit or meat cooked in a pastry case

piece pieces

a part of something larger

pier piers

a place for ships to moor, built out from the land into the water

pierce

pierces, piercing, pierced

to make a hole in something; to stab

pig pigs

an animal kept on a farm. Pork and bacon are made from pigs.

pigeon pigeons

a fat grey bird that makes soft noises and is often seen in towns

piglet piglets

a baby pig

pile piles

a heap

pilgrim pilgrims

a person who travels to visit a holy place

pill pills

a small ball of medicine for swallowing; a tablet

pillar pillars

an upright post, usually of stone, often used to hold up a part of a building

pillow pillows

a cushion to rest your head on in bed

pilot pilots

1 a person who flies a plane
2 a person who goes on board a ship to guide it into harbour

pimple pimples

a small spot on the skin

pin pins

a tiny piece of pointed metal that is thin and sharp, used for holding things together

pincers

1 a tool with jaws that grip when closed
2 the claws of a crab or lobster

pinch

pinches, pinching, pinched

1 to nip tightly with the fingers
2 a very small amount

pine

pines, pining, pined

1 to long for something or somebody very much
2 a tall tree on which cones grow

pineapple pineapples

a large juicy fruit grown in some hot countries

pink

a very light red colour

pint pints

a measure of liquids (the same as about half a litre)

pip pips

a small seed

pipe pipes

a tube to carry a gas or liquid from one place to another

pirate pirates

a sea robber

pit pits

a hole in the ground

pitch pitches

1 an area of ground for playing games on
2 to put up a tent
3 to throw

pity

pities, pitying, pitied

1 to feel sorry for somebody
2 something you are sorry about

pizza pizzas

a flat open pie, topped with cheese, tomatoes or other foods and eaten hot

a
b
c
d
e
f
g
h
i
j
k
l
m
n
o
p P
q
r
s
t
u
v
w
x
y
z

a
b
c
d
e
f
g
h
i
j
k
l
m
n
o
p P
q
r
s
t
u
v
w
x
y
z

place places

a space for something

plague plagues

1 a terrible disease that spreads very quickly
2 the special name for a group of locusts

plaice plaice

a flat sea fish, used as food

plain

plainer, plainest

1 ordinary; simple
2 a flat piece of land

plait (say 'pl**at**')

plaits, plaiting, plaited

to twist together three or more strands of hair or rope, one strand over another

plan

plans, planning, planned

1 to arrange
2 a drawing or map of something

plane planes

see aeroplane

planet planets

one of the large objects that go round the sun (for example, the earth)

plank planks

a long flat piece of wood

plant plants

1 something that grows in soil
2 to put something into soil to grow

plaster plasters

a strip of sticky material that you put over a cut on your skin

plastic plastics

a light and strong manufactured material used to make many different objects

plate plates

a flat dish from which you eat

platform platforms

1 a raised place, usually in a hall
2 the place in a station where you get on and off trains

play

plays, playing, played

1 to do something for fun (for example, sports or games)
2 to make music with an instrument (for example, a piano)
3 a story that is acted

playground playgrounds

a place for children to play, often with swings and slides

playgroup playgroups

a group of young children who play together, with adults looking after them

pleasant

more pleasant, most pleasant

nice; pleasing; making you happy

please

pleases, pleasing, pleased

1 to make someone happy
2 the word you use when you ask for something

pleasure pleasures

happiness; joy

pleat pleats

a fold that stays pressed into a piece of clothing

plenty

more than enough

pliers

a tool with handles and a head for gripping and cutting things

plot plots

1 what happens in a story
2 a piece of ground
3 a secret plan

plough ploughs

a machine for breaking up the soil

pluck

plucks, plucking, plucked

1 to take the feathers from a dead bird
2 to gather (flowers, for example)
3 to pull and then let go (for example, the strings of a guitar)

plug plugs

1 a stopper for a bath or a bowl
2 a fitting you put into a socket to get electricity

plum plums

a soft red or purple fruit with a large hard seed called a stone inside it

plumber plumbers

a person who fits and repairs water pipes

plump

plumper, plumpest

a bit fat; rounded

plunge

plunges, plunging, plunged

to dive in

plural plurals

more than one

plus

added to; the sign +

p.m.

the time between noon and midnight; afternoon; evening

poach

poaches, poaching, poached

1 to cook gently in water (for example, an egg)
2 to hunt animals or catch fish without permission

pocket pockets

a small bag sewn into clothes to hold money and other things

pod pods

in some plants, this is the part that contains the seeds

poem poems

a piece of poetry

poet poets

a person who writes poems

poetry

words written in lines of a certain length and often rhyming at the end

p P

a
b
c
d
e
f
g
h
i
j
k
l
m
n
o
p P
q
r
s
t
u
v
w
x
y
z

point

points, pointing, pointed

1 to show with a finger
2 the sharp end
3 a dot
4 a certain place or time

poison poisons

something that can harm or kill you if it gets into your body

poisonous

containing poison

poke

pokes, poking, poked

to push with a stick or finger

polar

to do with the North Pole or the South Pole, the two points on the earth's surface furthest from the equator

polar bear polar bears

a large white bear that lives near the North Pole

pole poles

a long rounded stick

police

the people whose job it is to make sure that the law is obeyed

polish

polishes, polishing, polished

1 to make smooth and bright by rubbing
2 a substance used for polishing

polite

well behaved; not rude

pollen

fine yellow dust found in flowers. It is carried to other flowers to make seeds.

polythene

a kind of plastic

pond ponds

a small lake

pony ponies

a small horse

poodle poodles

a kind of dog kept as a pet

pool pools

1 a place for playing or swimming in water
2 a small pond

poor

poorer, poorest

1 not having much money; not rich
2 not very good

pop pops

1 a soft sudden noise
2 a fizzy drink
3 popular music

popcorn

a snack made of corn with salt or sugar. It is often eaten at the cinema.

poppadom poppadoms

a thin round piece of dough, fried in oil. This is an Asian food.

poppy poppies

a wild plant with large flowers, often red

popular

well liked by people

population populations

the people who live in a particular place

porch porches

a shelter over the outside door of a building

pork

meat from a pig

porpoise porpoises

a sea animal rather like a dolphin

porridge

a breakfast food made of oats cooked in water or milk

port ports

a place where ships take on and drop off their cargo

portable

able to be carried about

porthole portholes

an opening in a ship's side to let in air and light

portion portions

a part or a share of something

portrait portraits

a picture of a person (it could be a drawing, a painting or a photograph)

position positions

1 the place where something or somebody is
2 a job

positive

certain; quite sure

possess

possesses, possessing, possessed

to have; to own

possible

able to be done; may take place but not definitely

post posts

1 a thick upright pole fixed in the ground
2 the sending and delivering of letters, parcels and postcards
3 a job; a position
4 to put on the internet

postcard postcards

a card with a photo on it, which you send when you are on holiday

poster posters

a large piece of paper with a message or a picture on it, which is put up in a public place

postman postmen
postwoman postwomen

the person who collects and delivers your mail

pot pots

a deep round container; some pots are used for cooking

potato potatoes

an oval or round vegetable grown under the ground

pottery

pots and dishes made of baked clay

a b c d e f g h i j k l m n o p P q r s t u v w x y z

a
b
c
d
e
f
g
h
i
j
k
l
m
n
o
p P
q
r
s
t
u
v
w
x
y
z

pouch pouches

a small bag

pound pounds

1 an amount of British money
   equal to 100 pence (£)
2 to beat very hard

pour

pours, pouring, poured

1 to make liquid flow out of a
   container
2 to rain heavily

powder powders

dust made by crushing a hard
material

power

strength; force

powerful

strong; forceful

practice

doing something often in order to
get better at it

practise

practises, practising, practised

to do something often in order to
get better at it

praise

praises, praising, praised

to say good things about a person

pram prams

a small carriage for a baby or doll

prawn prawns

a kind of small shellfish

pray

prays, praying, prayed

to speak to God

prayer prayers

the words you say when praying

preach

preaches, preaching, preached

to give a religious talk

precious

very valuable; much loved

predict

predicts, predicting, predicted

to say what will happen in the
future

prefer

prefers, preferring, preferred

to like one person or thing more
than the others

preparations

the things you do to get ready

prepare

prepares, preparing, prepared

to make something (such as a
meal) or get ready for something

pre-school pre-schools

a place where children can go
to learn and play when they are
three years old

present (say 'present')
presents

1 a gift
2 in a place or with people
3 **at present** now

present (say 'present')
presents, presenting, presented

to hand something over to
someone else

presently

in a short time; soon

preserve

preserves, preserving, preserved

to keep something from harm or from going bad

president presidents

the head of a country or of an organisation

press

presses, pressing, pressed

1 to push hard
2 to make smooth with an iron
3 a machine for printing

pretend

pretends, pretending, pretended

1 to act as though you were somebody or something else
2 to act as though something is true when it is not

pretty

prettier, prettiest

pleasant to see; looking nice

prevent

prevents, preventing, prevented

to stop something from taking place

previous

coming before

prey prey

1 a bird or animal that is hunted and killed by other creatures for food
2 bird of prey a large bird that kills and eats smaller birds and animals

price prices

what you must pay to buy something; the cost

priceless

very valuable

prick

pricks, pricking, pricked

to make a small hole with something pointed

prickly

pricklier, prickliest

1 having sharp points or thorns (as on a holly leaf, for example)
2 bad tempered; easily annoyed

pride

1 the feeling or belief that you are better than other people in some way
2 the special name for a group of lions

priest priests

a person whose job it is to perform religious duties

prim

primmer, primmest

easily shocked; almost too well-behaved

primary

first; earliest

prime minister

prime ministers

the head of a government

primrose primroses

a small wild plant that has yellow flowers in spring

a
b
c
d
e
f
g
h
i
j
k
l
m
n
o
p P
q
r
s
t
u
v
w
x
y
z

a
b
c
d
e
f
g
h
i
j
k
l
m
n
o
p P
q
r
s
t
u
v
w
x
y
z

prince princes

a man or boy in a royal family

princess princesses

a woman or girl in a royal family

principal principals

most important; chief; head

principle principles

a rule that we keep or live by

print

prints, printing, printed

1 to press letters onto paper using a machine
2 to write without joining up the letters

printer printers

1 a machine that prints things
2 a person who operates a printing machine

prison prisons

a place where people who have broken the law are kept

prisoner prisoners

a person who has been sent to prison

private

belonging to one person or group only

prize prizes

a reward given if you are very good at something or if you are lucky

probable

likely

problem problems

a difficult thing to work out

procession processions

an orderly march

prod

prods, prodding, prodded

to poke with a stick or finger

produce (say 'produce')

something produced by growing

produce (say 'produce')

produces, producing, produced

1 to bring out; to show
2 to make

profit profits

money you make when you sell something for more than you paid for it; gain

program programs

instruction that tells a computer what to do

programme programmes

1 information about what will happen and when (for example, at a concert or a competition)
2 something broadcast on television or radio

progress (say 'progress')

moving forward; getting better

progress (say 'progress')

progresses, progressing, progressed

to go forward; to advance

prohibit

prohibits, prohibiting, prohibited

to forbid, usually by order

project projects

1 a plan for something special
2 a long piece of work (for example, finding information about a subject)

promise

promises, promising, promised

to say for certain that you will do something

prompt

in good time; at the right time

prong prongs

the sharp spike of a fork

pronoun pronouns

a word used in place of a noun (for example, he, she, it)

pronounce

pronounces, pronouncing, pronounced

to say a word in a certain way

proof

the thing that shows or proves something to be true

propeller propellers

curved blades on a ship or an aeroplane that drive it forward

proper

correct; right

property properties

something that belongs to someone

propose

proposes, proposing, proposed

to suggest; to offer

prosper

prospers, prospering, prospered

to do well; to succeed

protect

protects, protecting, protected

to prevent someone or something from being harmed or damaged

protest

protests, protesting, protested

to say strongly that you are against something

proud

prouder, proudest

being very pleased with something you own or have done because it is very good. You can also be proud of your close friends and relatives when they do good things.

prove

proves, proving, proved

to show that something is true

proverb proverbs

a short well-known saying

provide

provides, providing, provided

to give what is needed; to supply

prune prunes

a dried plum

psalm psalms

a poem or song from the Bible

pub pubs

a place where adults go to drink, eat or meet their friends

public

for everybody to use

a
b
c
d
e
f
g
h
i
j
k
l
m
n
o
p P
q
r
s
t
u
v
w
x
y
z

publish

publishes, publishing, published

to produce and send out things that people have written (for example, books, articles, newspapers)

pudding puddings

a sweet dish eaten at the end of a meal

puddle puddles

a small pool (of rain water, for example)

puff puffs

a short burst of breath or smoke

puffin puffins

a sea bird with a short thick beak

pull

pulls, pulling, pulled

to drag something towards you

pulp

anything that has been mashed until smooth, especially fruit or vegetables

pulse

the beating of the heart

pump

pumps, pumping, pumped

1 to force air or liquid into or along something
2 a machine that does this

pumpkin pumpkins

a large round orange vegetable

punch

punches, punching, punched

1 to hit with the fist
2 to make a hole in something

punctual

arriving at the exact time

punctuation

full stops, commas and other marks used in writing

puncture punctures

a small hole made by something pointed

punish

punishes, punishing, punished

to make someone unhappy because they have done something wrong

pupil pupils

a person who is being taught, especially in a school

puppet puppets

a kind of doll that can be made to move by pulling strings or by putting your hand inside

puppy puppies

a young dog

purchase

purchases, purchasing, purchased

to buy

pure

purer, purest

with nothing added

purple

a colour made by mixing red and blue

purpose purposes

1 what you mean to do
2 **on purpose** meaning to do something; not by accident

purse purses

a small bag for holding money

pursue

pursues, pursuing, pursued

to follow; to run after

push

pushes, pushing, pushed

to press against something to try to move it

pushchair pushchairs

a chair on wheels in which you push a baby or a small child; a buggy

put

puts, putting, put

to place something

putty

a soft mixture that hardens to hold glass in a frame

puzzle puzzles

1 something that is difficult to understand
2 a game that has to be carefully worked out

pyjamas

trousers and a top worn in bed

pylon pylons

a large metal tower that supports cables high up in the air

pyramid pyramids

a shape or building that has a flat bottom and triangular sides that meet in a point

python pythons

a large snake that squeezes its victims to death

When you see the letters '**qu**' at the beginning of a word, you usually say '**kw**'.

quack quacks

the noise made by ducks

quaint

quainter, quaintest

unusual; strange; odd

quality qualities

how good or bad something is

quantity quantities

amount

quarrel

quarrels, quarrelling, quarrelled

to disagree angrily with someone

quarry quarries

a place where stone is taken out of the ground

quarter quarters

one of the four equal parts of something

quay (here you say '**key**')

quays

a place for ships to moor

a b c d e f g h i j k l m n o p **q Q** r s t u v w x y z

a
b
c
d
e
f
g
h
i
j
k
l
m
n
o
p
q Q
r
s
t
u
v
w
x
y
z

queen queens

1 a woman who is the ruler of a country
2 the wife of a king

queer

queerer, queerest

strange; odd; peculiar

quench

quenches, quenching, quenched

1 to end someone's thirst
2 to put out a fire

query queries

a question, especially about something you think might be wrong

quest quests

a journey, especially to find or achieve something

question questions

something that needs an answer

queue (here you say 'Q')

queues

a line of waiting people or vehicles

quiche (here you say 'keesh')

quiches

a tart with a filling made of eggs and often cheese

quick

quicker, quickest

fast; at great speed

quicksand

an area of sand that is very dangerous because you can sink into it

quiet

quieter, quietest

with very little or no sound

quill quills

1 a long feather
2 long ago, a pen made from such a feather

quilt quilts

a padded cover for the bed

quit

quits, quitting, quit

1 to leave; to exit, especially from a website or computer program
2 to give up, especially a game or competition

quite

1 completely; fully
2 a little, but not very much

quiver

quivers, quivering, quivered

1 to shake; to tremble
2 a holder for arrows

quiz quizzes

a game in which questions have to be answered

quotation marks

the punctuation marks used to show when a person starts and stops speaking

quote

quotes, quoting, quoted

to repeat exactly what someone has said or written

Qur'an (say 'Koran')

the religious book of Muslims

rR

rabbit rabbits

a small furry animal that lives in a hole in the ground

race races

1 a test of speed
2 people of the same kind

rack racks

a frame or bar for holding things

racket rackets

1 a kind of bat, but with strings instead of flat wood (used in tennis, for example)
2 a lot of very loud noise

radar

a way of helping to guide ships and aeroplanes by using radio waves

radiator radiators

1 a device that sends out heat
2 the front part of the engine of a car, which cools the engine

radio radios

a piece of equipment that receives special waves, which are turned into sounds for you to listen to

radish radishes

a small red or white sharp-tasting vegetable used in salads

radius radii

a straight line from the centre to the outside edge of a circle

raffia

straw made from large leaves that can be woven into mats and baskets

raffle raffles

a game of chance used to make money. Tickets with numbers are sold and some numbers win prizes.

raft rafts

a flat boat, often made of logs tied together

rafter rafters

a beam that holds up a roof

rag rags

a piece of cloth that is old or torn

rage rages

great anger; a violent temper

raid raids

a sudden unexpected attack

rail rails

a fixed wooden, plastic or metal bar

railway railways

everything to do with trains

rain

drops of water falling from the clouds

a b c d e f g h i j k l m n o p q **r R** s t u v w x y z

a
b
c
d
e
f
g
h
i
j
k
l
m
n
o
p
q
r R
s
t
u
v
w
x
y
z

rainbow rainbows

curved stripes of different colours, seen in the sky when the sun shines through rain

raise

raises, raising, raised

1 to lift up
2 to look after any living creature from the time when it is very young

raisin raisins

a dried grape

rake rakes

a garden tool with spikes for scratching the earth or gathering dead leaves

rally rallies

a large gathering of people

ram rams

1 a male sheep
2 to crash into

Ramadan

an important Muslim festival

ramble rambles

1 a long country walk
2 to talk in a muddled way and for a long time

ramp ramps

a slope between two levels

ranch ranches

a large cattle or sheep farm

random

1 in no special order
2 at random by chance

range ranges

1 the limit that something can reach
2 a variety of different things (for example, goods in a shop)
3 a row of mountains or hills

rank ranks

1 a line or row (for example, of soldiers)
2 a person's official position (for example, a captain in the army)

ransom ransoms

a sum of money paid to buy a prisoner's freedom

rap raps

a sharp blow or knock

rapid

very fast; very quick

rare

rarer, rarest

scarce; not often seen

rascal rascals

a badly-behaved child or a person who does bad things

rash

1 not thinking enough; doing things too quickly
2 a number of spots on the skin

raspberry raspberries

a small juicy berry that is dark red

rat rats

an animal like a large mouse

rate rates

1 the speed of something
2 the price that has been fixed

rather

1 more willingly; prefer to; sooner
2 quite; a little

rattle rattles

1 the noise of things being shaken together
2 a baby's toy that you shake

rave

raves, raving, raved

to speak wildly

raven ravens

a large black bird of the crow family

ravenous

very hungry

ravine ravines

a very deep and steep-sided narrow valley

raw

1 not cooked
2 very cold (weather)

ray rays

a beam or shaft of light

razor razors

a very sharp tool for shaving with

reach

reaches, reaching, reached

1 to stretch and touch
2 to arrive at; to get to

read

reads, reading, read

to understand the meaning of written or printed words

ready

1 willing to do something
2 prepared for use

real

true; not false

realise

realise, realising, realised

to come to understand something, especially suddenly

really

truly

reap

reaps, reaping, reaped

to cut and gather in a crop

rear

1 the back part
2 to look after children or small animals until they are fully grown
3 to stand up on the back legs (it is usually a horse that does this)

reason reasons

why something happens; the explanation

reasonable

sensible; not asking too much

rebel (say 'rebel') rebels

a person who rebels

rebel (say 'rebel')

rebels, rebelling, rebelled

to stop obeying orders

recall

recalls, recalling, recalled

1 to call back
2 to remember

a
b
c
d
e
f
g
h
i
j
k
l
m
n
o
p
q
r R
s
t
u
v
w
x
y
z

a
b
c
d
e
f
g
h
i
j
k
l
m
n
o
p
q

r R

s
t
u
v
w
x
y
z

receipt receipts

a piece of paper stating that something has been received

receive

receives, receiving, received

to take; to get something that is given or sent

recent

just happened

recipe recipes

a list of instructions telling you how to prepare a particular dish

recite

recites, reciting, recited

to say aloud from memory

reckon

reckons, reckoning, reckoned

1 to count; to add up
2 to think

record (say 'record')

1 the best that has been done so far
2 something written down to tell you what has happened

record (say 'record')

records, recording, recorded

1 to put voices or music on a disk so that you can listen to them again
2 to write down

recorder recorders

a wooden or plastic musical instrument played by blowing

recover

recovers, recovering, recovered
1 to get better after an illness
2 to get something back

re-cover

re-covers, re-covering, re-covered

to put a new cover on

recreation recreations

rest or play after you have been working

rectangle rectangles

a flat shape with two sides longer than the other two, like this page

recycle

recycles, recycling, recycled

to separate your rubbish so that some of it (glass or paper, for example) can be used again to make new things

red

the colour of blood

reduce

reduces, reducing, reduced

to make something less or smaller

reed reeds

a kind of long thin plant that grows near water

reef reefs

a line of rocks just below the level of the sea

reel reels

1 a cylinder used for winding something onto (for example, a fishing reel, a reel of cotton)
2 a lively Scottish dance
3 to stagger about

refer (to)

refers, referring, referred

1 to talk about; to mention
2 to be concerned with

referee referees

the person who makes sure that a game is played fairly

reference book
reference books

a book you can look things up in (a dictionary or an atlas, for example)

reflect

reflects, reflecting, reflected

1 to show or shine back, like a mirror
2 to think about something that has happened

refreshments

things to eat or drink

refrigerator (fridge)
refrigerators (fridges)

a special kind of container for keeping food cold

refuse (say 'ref**use**')

rubbish

refuse (say 'ref**use**')
refuses, refusing, refused

not to accept; to say 'No'

regard

regards, regarding, regarded

to look at

regiment regiments

a large group of soldiers; a part of an army

region regions

a part of the world or of a country

register registers

a list of names kept for a special purpose

regret

regrets, regretting, regretted

to be very sorry about; to wish that something hadn't happened

regular

happening often at the same time; usual

rehearse

rehearses, rehearsing, rehearsed

to practise something (for a play or a concert, for example)

reign

reigns, reigning, reigned

1 to rule as a king or queen
2 the length of time a king or queen reigns

reindeer reindeer

a kind of deer with long horns, which lives in cold northern countries

reins

straps used to control and guide an animal (or sometimes a small child)

relation relations

someone in the same family

relative relatives

someone in the same family

relay relays

a race in which each person in a team runs or swims a different part of the course

a b c d e f g h i j k l m n o p q **r R** s t u v w x y z

a
b
c
d
e
f
g
h
i
j
k
l
m
n
o
p
q
r R
s
t
u
v
w
x
y
z

release

releases, releasing, released

to allow to go free

reliable

able to be trusted

relic relics

a thing left from past times, sometimes thought to be holy

relief

1 the feeling when pain, fear or worry stops
2 help for people in trouble

religion religions

a way of believing in a god

religious

to do with religion; following a religion

rely on

relies, relying, relied

to depend on; to count on; to trust

remain

remains, remaining, remained

to stay; not to go

remainder

what is left over

remark remarks

something said about someone or something

remarkable

unusual; worth noticing

remedy remedies

a cure

remember

remembers, remembering, remembered

to bring back into the mind; not to forget

remind

reminds, reminding, reminded

to make someone remember

removal removals

moving from one house or flat to another

remove

removes, removing, removed

1 to take away
2 to move from one place to another

rent

the money you pay to use something that belongs to someone else

repair

repairs, repairing, repaired

to mend; to put right

repeat

repeats, repeating, repeated

to do or say something again

replace

replaces, replacing, replaced

to put back

reply

replies, replying, replied

to answer

report reports

a description of something that has happened

reptile reptiles

an animal with scales that has lungs for breathing with and lays its eggs on land (for example, a snake or a lizard)

request

requests, requesting, requested

to ask politely for something

require

requires, requiring, required

to need; to want

rescue

rescues, rescuing, rescued

to save; to take out of danger

reserve

reserves, reserving, reserved

1 to keep something until it is needed
2 something spare or extra
3 an area of land set aside for wildlife

reservoir reservoirs

a large lake that has been specially made to supply a town or city with water

respect

respects, respecting, respected

to admire; to look up to

rest

1 the others; what is left over
2 to be still; not to work or do anything tiring

restaurant restaurants

a place where you can buy and eat a meal

restore

restores, restoring, restored

1 to give back; to bring back
2 to clean and repair

result results

1 what happens because of something else
2 the final score in a game

retire

retires, retiring, retired

to stop working, usually because you have reached a certain age

retreat

retreats, retreating, retreated

to go back, especially if in danger

return

returns, returning, returned

1 to go or come back to a place
2 to give back

reveal

reveals, revealing, revealed

to show; to make known, especially something hidden

revenge

the hurt you do to someone in return for something they did to you

reverse

reverses, reversing, reversed

1 to go backwards
2 to go in the opposite direction

revise

revises, revising, revised

1 to read something and then correct and improve it
2 to look over something again to remind yourself about it (for example, before a test)

a
b
c
d
e
f
g
h
i
j
k
l
m
n
o
p
q
r R
s
t
u
v
w
x
y
z

revolt

revolts, revolting, revolted

to turn against a leader

revolution revolutions

a great change, especially a change in the government of a country made by force

reward rewards

something you are given for something good or brave you have done

rhinoceros (rhino) rhinoceroses (rhinos)

a large animal with one or two horns on its nose

rhubarb (say 'roobarb')

a garden plant with juicy stalks that can be cooked and eaten

rhyme rhymes

1 word endings that sound alike
2 a short poem with rhymes in it

rhythm rhythms

the steady beat or sound pattern of poetry or music

rib ribs

one of the curved bones that go across your chest

ribbon ribbons

a narrow piece of material

rice

a plant grown in some hot countries; you can cook and eat the seeds

rich

richer, richest

having a lot of money or other valuable things

rid

rids, ridding, rid

to be free of

riddle riddles

1 a word puzzle
2 a question that has a funny answer, like a joke

ride

rides, riding, rode

to move about in a vehicle or on an animal such as a horse

ridiculous

so silly that it might make you laugh

right

1 correct; not wrong
2 good; true
3 the opposite of left
4 **right angle** a turn of 90 degrees

rim rims

the edge of something round, such as a bowl or a wheel

rind rinds

the outer covering (for example, of an orange, a lemon or a cheese)

ring rings

1 a circle
2 the sound made by a bell
3 a circle of metal worn on the finger as jewellery

rink rinks

a place made specially for ice-skating or roller-skating

rinse

rinses, rinsing, rinsed

to wash with clean water, usually after washing with soap

riot riots

fighting and disturbance by a lot of people

rip

rips, ripping, ripped

to tear roughly

ripe

riper, ripest

fully grown; ready to eat

ripple ripples

a tiny wave

rise

rises, rising, rose

1 to get up
2 to go higher

risk risks

the danger of something going wrong

rival rivals

a person who tries to equal or to do better than another person

river rivers

a long and wide stream of water, usually flowing into the sea

road roads

a wide hard track on which vehicles can travel

roam

roams, roaming, roamed

to wander about

roar roars

a loud and deep sound (for example, the sound a lion makes)

roast

roasts, roasting, roasted

to cook in fat in an oven or over a fire

rob

robs, robbing, robbed

to take something that does not belong to you; to steal from

robber robbers

a person who steals; a thief

robbery robberies

the act of robbing

robe robes

a long and loose piece of clothing

robin robins

a small brown bird with a red front

robot robots

a machine that can do some of the work a person can do

rock rocks

1 stone; a large piece of stone
2 to move from side to side
3 a long and sticky sweet that is shaped like a stick
4 a style of music

rockery rockeries

part of a garden with lots of rocks, where certain plants grow well

a
b
c
d
e
f
g
h
i
j
k
l
m
n
o
p
q
r R
s
t
u
v
w
x
y
z

rocket rockets

1 a kind of firework
2 a spaceship
3 a vegetable used in salads

rod rods

a thin bar of wood or metal

rogue rogues

a wicked person that you cannot trust

roll

rolls, rolling, rolled

1 to turn over and over
2 something rolled into a cylinder shape
3 a long sound made by drums
4 a kind of bread made from small pieces of dough

roller blade roller blades
roller skate roller skates

a boot or shoe with wheels attached, to let you move quickly over smooth ground

roof roofs

the top covering of a building

rook rooks

1 a black bird of the crow family with a grey beak
2 a chess piece, also called a castle

room rooms

1 a part of a building, with its own floor, walls and ceiling
2 space for something

root roots

1 the part of a plant that is in the soil and takes in water
2 the beginning or origin of something (for example, a problem)

rope ropes

a thick cord

rose roses

a plant with scented flowers and with thorns on its stem

rosy

rosier, rosiest

pink in colour

rot

rots, rotting, rotted

to go bad and die

rotten

1 gone bad
2 nasty; unpleasant

rough

rougher, roughest

1 not smooth; coarse
2 wild and stormy

round

the same shape as a ball or ring

rounders

a game played by two sides with a bat and ball

route routes

the way you take from one place to another

routine routines

things done in a regular orderly way

row (sounds like 'low') rows

1 a line of people or things
2 to move a boat using oars

row (sounds like 'now') rows

a noisy quarrel

rowing boat rowing boats

a boat that is moved using oars

royal

to do with kings and queens

rub

rubs, rubbing, rubbed

to move one thing against another
many times

rubber

1 elastic material made from the
  sap of the rubber tree
2 a small piece of rubber used for
  getting rid of marks on paper
  (also called an **eraser**)

rubbish

1 things that are of no use; waste
2 nonsense

ruby rubies

a deep-red precious stone

rucksack rucksacks

a bag you can carry on your back;
a backpack

rude

ruder, rudest

not polite

rug rugs

1 a small carpet; a mat
2 a kind of blanket

rugby

a game played with an oval ball
that may be kicked or carried

ruin ruins

1 a building that has fallen down
2 to wreck; to spoil

rule rules

1 a law that must be followed
2 to be in charge; to make rules
  that tell people what to do

ruler rulers

1 a person whose job it is to tell
  other people what to do (for
  example, a king is a ruler)
2 a strip of plastic, wood or other
  material, used for measuring or
  drawing straight lines

rumble rumbles

a deep roll of sound like the sound
of thunder

rumour rumours

something you hear that may or
may not be true

run

runs, running, ran

1 to move very quickly on foot
2 to flow

rung rungs

a step on a ladder

rush

rushes, rushing, rushed

to move very quickly; to hurry

rust

a reddish-brown substance
sometimes found on iron and steel

rustle rustles

a gentle whispering sound, like the
sound of dry leaves moving

rye

a kind of grass. In some countries,
its grain is made into bread.

a
b
c
d
e
f
g
h
i
j
k
l
m
n
o
p
q
r **R**
s
t
u
v
w
x
y
z

a
b
c
d
e
f
g
h
i
j
k
l
m
n
o
p
q
r
s S
t
u
v
w
x
y
z

sS

Sabbath

the special day for worshipping God in the Jewish and Christian religions

sack sacks

1 a very large and strong bag
2 to remove somebody from a job

sacred

holy; to do with religion

sacrifice sacrifices

the giving up of something that you like very much

sad

sadder, saddest

unhappy; miserable

saddle saddles

the seat of a bicycle; a seat for the rider of a horse

safari safaris

a journey on which you are taken to see wild animals (especially in Africa)

safari park safari parks

a park where you can see wild animals wandering about

safe

safer, safest

1 not in danger
2 a strong metal box that may be locked, for keeping valuable things in

safety

a safe place

safety belt safety belts

a belt that holds you safely in a seat

sag

sags, sagging, sagged

to hang downwards, usually in the middle

sail sails

1 a large piece of strong cloth fixed onto a sailing boat. Wind fills the sail and moves the boat through the water.
2 to travel in a boat

sailor sailors

1 a person who works on a ship
2 a person who sails a yacht

saint saints

a very good and holy person

salad salads

a dish of vegetables eaten cold and usually raw

salary salaries

the money that someone is paid for the work they have done

sale sales

1 the selling of things
2 a time when things are sold at a lower price than usual

saliva

the liquid in your mouth; spit

salmon salmon

a large fish with pink flesh

salt

a white mineral that is made into powder and used to flavour or preserve food

salute

salutes, saluting, saluted

to greet, especially by raising the hand to the forehead

salwar kameez

loose trousers and a tunic, worn by some Asian women

same

not different; exactly like

sample samples

1 a small amount of something that shows what it is like
2 to test; to try out

sand

powdered rock or shells often found at the seaside or in the desert

sandal sandals

a shoe with an open top, fastened with straps or cords

sandwich sandwiches

two slices of bread with a filling between them

sane

saner, sanest

not mad; sensible

sap

1 the liquid in the stems of plants and trees
2 to weaken; to drain energy from something

sarcastic

being hurtful to someone by saying one thing but meaning the opposite

sardine sardines

a small sea fish used as food

sari saris

a type of dress worn by some Asian women, made of a long piece of material that is wrapped around the body

sash sashes

a long scarf worn round the waist or over the shoulder

satellite satellites

a natural or manufactured object moving in space round a planet (for example, the moon is the earth's satellite)

satellite dish

satellite dishes

a device designed to receive signals from satellites

satellite navigation

using information from satellites to help you find your way on a journey

satin

a kind of smooth cloth with one shiny side, usually made of silk

satisfy

satisfies, satisfying, satisfied

to give enough, so that the person you are giving to is content

a
b
c
d
e
f
g
h
i
j
k
l
m
n
o
p
q
r
s S
t
u
v
w
x
y
z

a b c d e f g h i j k l m n o p q r **s S** t u v w x y z

satsuma satsumas

a kind of fruit like a small orange

sauce sauces

a thick liquid food eaten with other food to add flavour

saucepan saucepans

a metal container with a handle, used for cooking

saucer saucers

a small round plate on which a cup stands

sausage sausages

minced meat in a thin skin

savage

fierce; wild; cruel

save

saves, saving, saved

1 to bring a person out of danger
2 to keep something until you need it

savings

money you have saved up

saw saws

1 a metal tool with sharp pointed teeth for cutting
2 to cut something with a saw (for example, wood)

say

says, saying, said

to speak

scab scabs

a hard covering that forms over a wound or spot

scaffolding

a framework made of poles and planks that builders climb up on when working on the outside of a building

scald

scalds, scalding, scalded

to burn with hot liquid

scale scales

1 a set of numbers or marks for measuring
2 a set of musical notes going up and down
3 a small piece of flat shiny material (on the skin of a fish or snake, for example)

scales

a machine for weighing people or things

scalp scalps

the skin on your head, underneath your hair

scamper

scampers, scampering, scampered

to run quickly and lightly

scandal scandals

something said or talked about that shocks other people

scar scars

a mark left on the skin by a wound that has healed

scarce

scarcer, scarcest

rare; not often found because only a few exist

scarcely

hardly at all

scare

scares, scaring, scared

to frighten

scared

frightened by someone or something

scarf scarves

a length of cloth used as a covering for the neck, shoulders or head

scarlet

a very bright red colour

scatter

scatters, scattering, scattered

1 to throw something about in different directions
2 to move away quickly in different directions

scene scenes

1 a view
2 a part of a play
3 the place where something happened

scent scents

1 a pleasant smell; a perfume
2 the smell that an animal leaves behind it

scheme schemes

a plan

school schools

a place where people, usually children, go to learn

schoolchild

schoolchildren

a child who goes to school

science sciences

knowledge of nature and how things are made; science is sometimes a school subject

scientist scientists

a person who studies science

scissors

a cutting tool with two blades fastened together in the middle

scold

scolds, scolding, scolded

to talk harshly to someone because they have done something wrong

scooter scooters

1 a board with two wheels and a long handle; you put one foot on the board, hold on to the handle and push yourself along with the other foot
2 a small motorbike

scorch

scorches, scorching, scorched

to burn something slightly, often making it brown; to singe

score

scores, scoring, scored

1 to count points, runs or goals in a test, game or competition
2 the number of points, runs or goals made in a test, game or competition

a
b
c
d
e
f
g
h
i
j
k
l
m
n
o
p
q
r
s **S**
t
u
v
w
x
y
z

scout scouts

1 a person who is sent to find out information (for example, about an enemy)
2 a Scout is a member of the Scouts, a club that provides adventure activities, usually for boys

scowl

scowls, scowling, scowled

to give a very angry look; to frown

scramble

scrambles, scrambling, scrambled

1 to climb or crawl quickly, often over rough ground
2 to mix up

scrap scraps

1 a tiny piece
2 rubbish thrown away
3 a fight

scrape

scrapes, scraping, scraped

1 to rub and clean with something hard
2 a difficulty

scratch

scratches, scratching, scratched

1 to mark with something pointed or sharp
2 to rub the skin because it is itchy

scrawl

scrawls, scrawling, scrawled

to write badly; to scribble

scream

screams, screaming, screamed

to make a shrill cry, usually because of fear or pain

screen screens

1 a large white surface on which a film is shown; the viewing part of a television set or computer
2 a large covered-in frame (for example, used as a shelter from sun or rain or to divide up a room)

screw screws

a metal nail with grooves round it; you turn it round and round to fix things together

scribble

scribbles, scribbling, scribbled

to write quickly and carelessly

scrub

scrubs, scrubbing, scrubbed

to clean with water, and usually a brush

scuffle scuffles

a struggle with much pushing; a kind of fight

sculptor sculptors

a person who makes artistic shapes out of stone, metal or other materials

sculpture sculptures

a shape made out of stone, metal or other materials

sea seas

the salt water that surrounds the land on the earth's surface

seal seals

1 a kind of sea animal with fur
2 to close or fasten tightly (for example, an envelope)

seam seams

1 a line of stitches where two pieces of cloth are joined
2 a layer of coal or other minerals under the ground

search

searches, searching, searched

to look very hard for something

seasick

feeling sick because of the movement of a boat or ship

seaside

an area of land that is right beside the sea

season seasons

1 one of the four main parts of the year: spring, summer, autumn or winter
2 a special time of year (for example, the holiday season)
3 to add something to food to make it taste better (for example, salt, pepper, herbs)

seat seats

something to sit on

seat belt seat belts

a belt you wear in a car, coach or aeroplane to stop you being thrown about if there is an accident

seaweed

plants that grow in the sea

second seconds

1 a very short period of time (there are 60 seconds in one minute)
2 after the first

second hand

not new; having been owned by someone else

secret secrets

something known about by only a few people

secretary secretaries

a person whose job it is to write letters and do office work for another person or for an organisation

section sections

a part of something

secure

firm; safe; free from danger

see

sees, seeing, saw

1 what you are able to do with your eyes
2 to understand

seed seeds

a grain from which a plant grows

seek

seeks, seeking, sought

to search for; to look for

seem

seems, seeming, seemed

to appear to be

seesaw seesaws

a playground toy. One child sits on each end of a plank of wood that is balanced in the middle on a special stand; when one child goes down, the other goes up.

a b c d e f g h i j k l m n o p q r **s S** t u v w x y z

seize

seizes, seizing, seized

to take hold of roughly; to grab quickly

seldom

not often; rarely

select

selects, selecting, selected

to choose; to pick out as you wish

selection selections

a number of things that have been chosen

selfish

thinking only about yourself

sell

sells, selling, sold

to give something to someone else, who gives you money for it

semicircle semicircles

half a circle

send

sends, sending, sent

to make someone or something go somewhere

senior

1 older than others
2 having a higher position in an organisation or having been there longer

sense senses

1 smell, sight, hearing, taste or touch
2 knowing the right thing to do

sensible

having good sense

sentence sentences

1 a group of words that make sense together
2 a punishment given by a judge at the end of a trial

sentry sentries

a soldier on guard at a door or gate

separate

1 not joined in any way
2 to take things apart so they are not joined any more

sequence sequences

the order that things come in (for example, numbers)

sergeant sergeants

an officer in the police or in the army

serial serials

a story told or written in parts

serious

1 very important
2 worrying or bad
3 not laughing or smiling very much

sermon sermons

a talk given as part of a service in a church

serpent serpents

a snake

servant servants

a person who does work for another person, especially cleaning and cooking

serve

serves, serving, served

to do things for other people (for example, to give them food and drink, or to help them buy things in a shop)

service services

1 something you do for others
2 something people can use to help them (for example, a bus service)
3 a special time in church, when people pray and sing together

set

sets, setting, set

1 to put something somewhere or to get it ready
2 a group of people or things that are alike in some way
3 what happens when some liquids cool and go solid (for example, jelly)

settee settees

a soft seat made for more than one person; a couch, a sofa

settle

settles, settling, settled

1 to sink to the bottom
2 to calm down; to be still

seven

7; a number

seventeen

17; a number

seventy

70; a number

several

some; a few; not many

severe

very serious or bad (for example, a severe delay is a long delay)

sew

sews, sewing, sewed

to join together with stitches using a needle and thread

sex sexes

one of the two groups, male and female, that people and animals belong to

shabby

shabbier, shabbiest

almost worn out

shade

1 a place where there is shelter from the sun or other strong light
2 how light or dark a colour is

shadow shadows

1 a dark shape seen where something comes between the light and a particular surface (for example, the ground)
2 a dark place where something is keeping out the light

shaft shafts

something long and straight, such as a long handle (for example, the handle of a spade) or a long space (for example, in a lift)

shake

shakes, shaking, shook

to move quickly from side to side; to shiver

a b c d e f g h i j k l m n o p q r s S t u v w x y z

a b c d e f g h i j k l m n o p q r s S t u v w x y z

shallow

shallower, shallowest

not deep

shame

a feeling of being unhappy because you have done wrong

shampoo shampoos

a special liquid soap that you use for washing your hair

shape shapes

the outline of something

share

shares, sharing, shared

1 to divide into parts
2 to use something along with someone else
3 a portion or part

shark sharks

a large fish with sharp teeth

sharp

sharper, sharpest

1 pointed; able to cut
2 quick; sudden
3 able to think, see or hear well and quickly
4 a sound that is just above the correct note in music

shave

shaves, shaving, shaved

to remove hair from the skin with a razor

shawl shawls

a piece of cloth used to cover the head and shoulders or to wrap around a baby

sheaf sheaves

a bundle of things tied together, especially newly cut corn

shears

a tool like big scissors, used outdoors

shed sheds

1 a small building
2 to take off, or let something fall off

sheep sheep

a farm animal with a woollen coat

sheet sheets

1 a large piece of cloth, often used on a bed
2 a thin and flat piece of material, such as paper, glass or metal

shelf shelves

a board fixed to a wall or inside a cupboard, for putting things on

shell shells

1 the hard covering of a sea creature, sometimes found on the beach
2 the hard covering of an egg, a nut or a seed

shellfish shellfish

a small sea creature that has a shell

shelter shelters

a place where you are protected from bad weather or danger

shepherd shepherds

a person who looks after sheep

shield

shields, shielding, shielded

1 to protect from harm
2 a large piece of metal or wood once used by soldiers to protect themselves

shift

shifts, shifting, shifted

to move

shin shins

the front of the leg between your knee and ankle

shine

shines, shining, shone

1 to give out light
2 to look bright; to sparkle

shingle

small stones or pebbles found at the seaside

ship ships

a very large boat

shipwreck shipwrecks

a ship that has been destroyed, usually by a storm

shirt shirts

a piece of clothing with sleeves and a collar, worn on the upper part of the body

shiver

shivers, shivering, shivered

to shake because of cold or fear

shoal shoals

a large group of fish of the same kind, all swimming together

shock shocks

1 something that upsets you because it is so sudden or because it gives you a nasty surprise
2 to make someone feel shock

shoe shoes

a covering for the foot that is made of leather or plastic and has a hard bottom

shoelace shoelaces

the special string used to tie your shoes or trainers

shoot

shoots, shooting, shot

1 to fire a weapon
2 new growth on a plant

shop

shops, shopping, shopped

1 to go to a shop to buy things
2 a place where things are sold

shopping

things that you buy in a shop

shore shores

the land along the edge of the sea or beside a lake

short

shorter, shortest

small from end to end; not long; not tall

shortage shortages

not enough

shorts

short trousers with legs that end above the knee

a b c d e f g h i j k l m n o p q r s S t u v w x y z

a
b
c
d
e
f
g
h
i
j
k
l
m
n
o
p
q
r
s S
t
u
v
w
x
y
z

shoulder shoulders

the place where the arm joins the body

shout

shouts, shouting, shouted

to speak or cry out in a loud voice

shove

shoves, shoving, shoved

to push hard

shovel shovels

a tool for lifting loose things (for example, coal)

show

shows, showing, showed

1 to allow to see
2 something you watch for fun (on television or at the theatre)

shower showers

1 a place to wash yourself where water sprays down on you from above
2 a short fall of rain or snow

shred shreds

a tiny narrow piece torn off something

shriek shrieks

a high-pitched scream of pain, surprise or laughter

shrill

shriller, shrillest

very high and piercing (usually used to describe a sound)

shrimp shrimps

a very small kind of shellfish

shrink

shrinks, shrinking, shrunk

to get smaller

shrub shrubs

a small tree or bush

shudder

shudders, shuddering, shuddered

to shake violently with fear or cold

shut

shuts, shutting, shut

1 to close
2 not open; closed

shuttlecock shuttlecocks

a piece of round cork or plastic with feathers. It is hit over a net in the game of badminton.

shy

shyer, shyest

afraid to speak; easily frightened

sick

sicker, sickest

1 bringing up food from the stomach
2 ill; not well

side sides

1 the part at the edge of something
2 the flat faces or lines between the corners of a shape
3 a team at games

sideways

moving to one side

siege sieges

the surrounding of a place by soldiers or police so that no help or food can reach it

sieve sieves

a utensil with small holes that let only liquid and tiny objects through

sigh

sighs, sighing, sighed

to make a low sound as you breathe out, because you are tired, sad or bored

sight

1 being able to see
2 something seen

sign signs

1 a mark, movement or message that tells you something
2 to write your name on

signal signals

a sign, sound or light that tells you something

signature signatures

your special way of writing your own name

Sikh (say '**seek**') Sikhs

a follower of a particular religion, especially in Northern India

silent

quiet; still; without noise; not saying anything

silk

a kind of smooth soft cloth

silly

sillier, silliest

foolish; stupid

silver

a valuable grey metal, used to make jewellery

similar

almost the same as something else

simple

simpler, simplest

1 plain; without any decoration
2 easy

sin

sins, sinning, sinned

to do something bad that is against the laws of a religion

since

1 from that time until now
2 because

sincere

meaning what you say; honest

sing

sings, singing, sang

to make music with the voice

singe

singes, singeing, singed

to burn slightly

single

1 only one
2 not married

sink

sinks, sinking, sank

1 to go down slowly, especially in water
2 a large fixed basin used for washing

sip

sips, sipping, sipped

to drink in tiny amounts

Sir

a polite title given to a man

a b c d e f g h i j k l m n o p q r **s S** t u v w x y z

siren sirens

a long and loud warning sound that can be heard from far away

sister sisters

a girl or woman who has the same parents as another person

sit

sits, sitting, sat

to rest on your bottom with your back upright

six

6; a number

sixteen

16; a number

sixty

60; a number

size sizes

how big something is

skate skates

1 a boot fitted with a metal blade that allows you to move quickly on ice
2 to move on ice using skates
3 to move on roller skates or roller blades

skateboard skateboards

a board with wheels underneath that you can stand on and do tricks on

skeleton skeletons

all the bones in the body

sketch

sketches, sketching, sketched

to draw quickly and roughly

ski skis

1 a long thin piece of wood, metal or plastic fitted to a boot to help you move quickly over snow
2 to move on snow using skis

skid

skids, skidding, skidded

to slide out of control on a slippery surface

skilful

having skill

skill

the ability to do something well

skin skins

the outer covering of a person, an animal, a fruit or a vegetable

skinny

skinnier, skinniest

very thin

skip

skips, skipping, skipped

1 to jump over a turning rope
2 to move with little jumping steps
3 a huge container for putting rubbish in

skirt skirts

a piece of clothing that hangs from the waist and is worn by women

skittle skittles

a wooden block knocked down by rolling or throwing a ball in the game of skittles

skull skulls

the bones that cover your head

sky skies

the place above the earth where you see the sun, moon and stars

skylark skylarks

a small bird that sings when it is flying high in the sky

skyscraper skyscrapers

a very tall building

slab slabs

a thick flat piece of something

slack

slacker, slackest

1 loose
2 careless; not working hard

slam

slams, slamming, slammed

to bang; to shut loudly

slant

slants, slanting, slanted

to slope

slap

slaps, slapping, slapped

to hit something or someone with the flat part of your hand

slate slates

1 a kind of grey rock that splits easily into thin pieces
2 a piece of this rock used as a tile on a roof

slaughter

slaughters, slaughtering, slaughtered

to kill animals for food

slave slaves

a person who is owned by another person and is forced to work for them without pay

slay

slays, slaying, slew

to kill

sledge sledges

a vehicle without wheels, specially made to slide smoothly over snow

sleep

sleeps, sleeping, slept

to rest your whole body with your eyes closed and without being conscious

sleet

snow and rain falling together

sleeve sleeves

the part of a piece of clothing that covers an arm

sleigh (say 'slay') sleighs

a sledge pulled along by animals

slice slices

a thin piece that is cut from something larger (for example, bread)

slide slides

1 a smooth surface made specially for sliding down, often found in playgrounds
2 to move smoothly along a slippery surface; to slip
3 a piece of plastic or metal that can be used to fasten your hair

slight

1 thin; small; not very strong
2 of little importance

slightly

a little

a b c d e f g h i j k l m n o p q r **s S** t u v w x y z

slim
slimmer, slimmest
1 thin
2 to make a special effort to become thinner

sling slings
1 a bandage to support a broken arm
2 to throw

slip
slips, slipping, slipped
1 to move quickly and quietly
2 to lose your balance on a smooth surface
3 to make a small mistake
4 a small piece of paper

slippers
light soft shoes worn indoors

slippery
so wet, greasy or smooth that it is difficult to hold or walk on

slit slits
a narrow cut or tear

slope slopes
a piece of ground that is higher at one end than at the other

slow
slower, slowest
taking a long time; not quick

slug slugs
a small animal like a snail, but without a shell

slush
half-melted watery snow

sly
slyer, slyest
not to be trusted; crafty; cunning

smack
smacks, smacking, smacked
to hit with a flat hand

small
smaller, smallest
little; not big

smart
smarter, smartest
1 clever; quick to understand
2 well dressed
3 to have a stinging feeling

smash
smashes, smashing, smashed
to break into many pieces

smear
smears, smearing, smeared
to spread a surface with something dirty, sticky or greasy

smell
smells, smelling, smelled, smelt
1 to notice something by using your nose
2 to have a smell

smile smiles
a happy look

smoke
the dark cloud that rises from something burning

smooth
smoother, smoothest
flat; not rough

smoothie smoothies

a drink made from fruit or vegetables blended together

smother

smothers, smothering, smothered

to stop someone breathing by covering his or her nose and mouth

smoulder

smoulders, smouldering, smouldered

to burn slowly with a lot of smoke but no flame

smudge smudges

a dirty mark that is usually made when you are writing

smuggle

smuggles, smuggling, smuggled

to take things into or out of a country secretly

snack snacks

a small amount of food eaten between meals

snail snails

a small slow-moving animal with a shell on its back

snake snakes

a smooth and legless animal that glides along on its body

snap

snaps, snapping, snapped

1 to bite at something quickly
2 to break with a sharp noise
3 to make a sharp noise with the fingers

snare snares

a trap set to catch animals

snarl

snarls, snarling, snarled

1 to growl showing the teeth
2 to speak in an angry way

snatch

snatches, snatching, snatched

to grab quickly

sneak

sneaks, sneaking, sneaked

to move secretly

sneer

sneers, sneering, sneered

to show that you do not think much of someone or something

sneeze sneezes

a sudden and noisy rush of air from the nose

sniff

sniffs, sniffing, sniffed

to smell noisily with quick breaths

snob snobs

a person who thinks too much about money and position

snore

snores, snoring, snored

to breathe heavily and noisily while asleep

snow

frozen water that falls in white flakes

snug

snugger, snuggest

warm; cosy; comfortable

a
b
c
d
e
f
g
h
i
j
k
l
m
n
o
p
q
r
s S
t
u
v
w
x
y
z

soak

soaks, soaking, soaked

1 to make very wet
2 to leave in liquid for a time

soap soaps

a fatty substance that is used with water for washing

sob

sobs, sobbing, sobbed

to weep noisily

sock socks

a covering for your foot and ankle

socket sockets

a hole into which something fits (for example, an electrical plug)

sofa sofas

a soft chair for more than one person; a couch or settee

soft

softer, softest

1 not hard
2 gentle; not rough
3 quiet; not loud

soil

1 the earth in which plants grow
2 to make dirty

soldier soldiers

a member of an army

sole soles

1 the bottom part of your foot or of a shoe or boot
2 a kind of flat fish

solemn

very serious

solid

1 hard; firm; not liquid or gas
2 not hollow

solo solos

something done by one person alone (for example, a piece of music played by just one person)

solve

solves, solving, solved

to find the answer to a problem

someone

a person that you do not know; any person

somersault

somersaults, somersaulting, somersaulted

to turn head over heels

son sons

a male child of a parent

song songs

a piece of music for the voice, with words as well as a tune

soon

sooner, soonest

in a short time

sooner

1 earlier
2 rather; prefer to

soot

the black substance left behind after burning (in a chimney, for example)

sore

painful

sorrow sorrows

a feeling of sadness

sorry

feeling unhappy because of something you have done or something that has happened

sort sorts

1 a kind; a type
2 to put into order

soul souls

the part of a person that is not the body or the mind and is thought to live on after death; the spirit

sound sounds

1 something you hear; a noise
2 strong and healthy; in a good state

soup soups

a liquid food made by boiling vegetables, meat or fish in water

sour

1 having a sharp and bitter taste, like a lemon
2 not fresh (of milk, for example)

source sources

a place where something starts (for example, a river)

south

the direction that is on the right as you face the rising sun

souvenir souvenirs

something you keep to remind you of something (a place you visit, for example)

sovereign sovereigns

a king or queen

sow (sounds like 'low')
sows, sowing, sowed

to put seeds into the ground so that they will grow

sow (sounds like 'now') sows

a female pig

space spaces

1 the distance between things
2 the place beyond the earth's atmosphere

spaceship spaceships

a vehicle made to travel in space

spade spades

1 a tool made for digging soil
2 one of the four kinds in a pack of playing cards

spaghetti

long strings of pasta

spanner spanners

a tool that turns a metal nut to tighten or loosen it

spare

not in use at present; extra

spark sparks

a tiny piece of burning material

sparkle

sparkles, sparkling, sparkled

to shine with tiny movements of light

sparrow sparrows

a small brown bird, often seen near houses

a
b
c
d
e
f
g
h
i
j
k
l
m
n
o
p
q
r
s S
t
u
v
w
x
y
z

speak

speaks, speaking, spoke

to use the voice to say something; to talk

spear spears

a weapon with a long thin handle and a sharp point

special

1 of a kind that is different
2 made or done for one person or occasion

speck specks

a tiny spot of something

spectacles

glasses to help you to see better

spectator spectators

a person who watches something (for example, a football match)

speech

the sounds that you make when you speak

speed speeds

the quickness or slowness with which something is done

spell

spells, spelling, spelled, spelt

1 to arrange letters one by one to make words
2 magic words that make things happen in stories

spend

spends, spending, spent

1 to give money to pay for something
2 to use time in doing something

sphere spheres

a round ball; a globe

spice spices

something used to give food a special taste (for example, pepper)

spider spiders

a small creature with eight legs that weaves a web to catch insects for food

spike spikes

a pointed object, especially of metal

spill

spills, spilling, spilled, spilt

to let a liquid or powder out of its container by accident

spin

spins, spinning, spun

1 to turn round and round very quickly
2 to make cotton or wool into thread

spinach

a kind of green vegetable

spine spines

the backbone

spire spires

the pointed upper part of a tower, often of a church

spirit spirits

1 the soul of a person
2 a ghost
3 life; energy

spit

1 saliva; the liquid that forms in your mouth
2 to force something out of your mouth

splash

splashes, splashing, splashed

to throw or scatter liquid noisily

splendid

1 excellent; very good
2 very grand

splinter splinters

a small sharp piece, usually of wood

split

splits, splitting, split

to crack; to break something along its length

spoil

spoils, spoiling, spoiled, spoilt

to ruin; to damage

spoilt

having been given everything you want so that you become badly behaved

spoke spokes

a thin bar from the centre of a wheel to the rim

sponge sponges

1 a soft object that soaks up water, used for washing
2 a soft light cake

spoon spoons

a tool used for eating or stirring soft foods or liquids

sport sports

games played for exercise or pleasure

spot spots

1 a tiny mark
2 to notice

spout spouts

a short tube or opening through which a liquid is poured (from a kettle or teapot, for example)

sprain

sprains, spraining, sprained

to injure by twisting badly (for example, the ankle or the wrist)

sprawl

sprawls, sprawling, sprawled

to spread your limbs out lazily

spray sprays

1 thin jets of water
2 a small bunch of flowers

spread

spreads, spreading, spread

1 to scatter about
2 to cover a surface with something
3 a food made from vegetable oils, often used instead of butter

spring

springs, springing, sprang

1 to jump in the air
2 a coiled piece of metal that jumps back when you press it down
3 a place where water appears from below the ground
4 the season between winter and summer

sprinkle

sprinkles, sprinkling, sprinkled

to scatter in small drops or grains

sprint

sprints, sprinting, sprinted

to run quickly for a short distance

sprout

sprouts, sprouting, sprouted

to begin to grow

spur spurs

1 a sharp instrument on a horse rider's heel, used to make the horse go faster
2 **spur on** to encourage a person or an animal to make more effort

spy spies

a person who finds and passes on information secretly

squabble

squabbles, squabbling, squabbled

to quarrel noisily about small things

square squares

a shape with four equal sides, like this ■

squash

squashes, squashing, squashed

1 to crush; to squeeze tightly together
2 a fruit drink that you add water to

squeak squeaks

a small sharp noise like the sound made by a mouse

squeal squeals

a long shrill cry, often caused by pain or joy

squeeze

squeezes, squeezing, squeezed

to press together; to squash

squirm

squirms, squirming, squirmed

to twist about; to wriggle

squirrel squirrels

a small animal with a bushy tail that lives among trees

stab

stabs, stabbing, stabbed

to make a wound with a sharp pointed weapon

stable stables

a building where horses are kept

stack stacks

a large and tidy pile

stadium stadiums

a large open-air sports ground with rows of seats

staff

a group of people who work together

stag stags

a male deer

stage stages

a raised platform in a building or hall

stagger

staggers, staggering, staggered

to walk unsteadily

stain stains

a mark that spoils something

stairs

a set of steps leading to another floor in a building

stale

staler, stalest

1 not fresh; no longer fit to eat
2 no longer interesting

stalk stalks

1 the stem of a flower or plant
2 to follow quietly an animal or a person

stall stalls

1 a counter for selling things (in a market, for example)
2 a place where a cow or horse is kept
3 **the stalls** seats on the ground level of a cinema or theatre

stallion stallions

a male horse

stammer

stammers, stammering, stammered

to have difficulty in saying words; to hesitate and repeat words without meaning to; to stutter

stamp stamps

1 the little piece of paper that you stick on a letter or parcel. It shows that you have paid to send it by post.
2 to put your feet down hard and noisily

stand

stands, standing, stood

1 to be upright
2 to rise up

standard standards

1 a level of measurement or ability
2 usual; with nothing extra

star stars

1 one of the tiny-looking bright objects seen in the sky at night
2 a very famous person, such as an actor, a singer or a footballer

starch

a white substance found in some foods (potatoes, for example)

stare

stares, staring, stared

to look at something steadily for a long time

starling starlings

a noisy bird with dark shiny feathers

start

starts, starting, started

to begin

startle

startles, startling, startled

to surprise or frighten

starve

starves, starving, starved

to be ill or die because you have no food

state

states, stating, stated

1 to say in words, by writing or by speaking
2 the condition of a thing or person
3 a country or its government
4 a part of certain countries, such as the United States of America

a
b
c
d
e
f
g
h
i
j
k
l
m
n
o
p
q
r
s S
t
u
v
w
x
y
z

statement statements

something said or written down, especially for an important reason

station stations

1 a place where trains stop
2 a building where certain services are provided (for example, a police station)

stationery

writing materials such as paper, envelopes and pens

statue statues

an image or a likeness in wood or stone

stay

stays, staying, stayed

not to go away; to remain

steady

steadier, steadiest

not moving; not changing; not too fast

steak steaks

a thick piece of meat or fish

steal

steals, stealing, stole

to take something that is not yours; to rob

steam

the mist or cloud that comes from boiling or very hot water

steel

a hard and strong metal that is made from iron

steep

steeper, steepest

sloping sharply

steeple steeples

a pointed tower on top of a church

steer

steers, steering, steered

to make a car or some other vehicle go the way you want it to

stem stems

the thin part of a plant on which the leaves or flowers grow

step

steps, stepping, stepped

1 to put one foot in front of the other when you walk or run
2 a flat place at a different level from the floor, where you put your feet to move either up or down (for example, on stairs)

stepfamily stepfamilies

the new family that is made when a divorced or widowed parent gets married again (for example, stepfather, stepmother, stepbrother, stepsister, stepdaughter, stepson)

stern

sterner, sternest

1 strict; harsh
2 the back part of a boat

stew stews

meat and vegetables cooked slowly in water

stick sticks

1 a short thin piece of wood
2 to fasten together with glue
3 **to stick out** to be longer than the things around or beneath

sticky
stickier, stickiest

able to stick to something else

stiff
stiffer, stiffest

hard; difficult to bend

stile stiles

steps for climbing over a fence

still
stiller, stillest

1 not moving; quiet
2 the same now as before

sting stings

the sharp pain you get when an insect, an animal or a plant pricks your skin

stir
stirs, stirring, stirred

1 to move something round and round with a stick or a spoon
2 to begin to move after being still for quite a long time

stirrups

the metal rings that hang from a saddle and into which a horse rider puts his or her feet

stitch stitches

1 a loop of thread made in sewing or knitting
2 a sudden pain in the side

stock

1 a quantity of things or animals
2 a liquid made by boiling meat, bones or vegetables. It is used to make soups and sauces.

stomach (tummy)
stomachs (tummies)

the place where your food goes after you swallow it

stone stones

1 a hard material found on and below the surface of the earth
2 a precious jewel
3 a hard seed found in some kinds of fruit

stool stools

a seat without a back

stoop
stoops, stooping, stooped

to bend your body forward

stop
stops, stopping, stopped

to end doing something

store stores

1 a place for keeping things
2 to save something for later
3 a large shop

storey storeys

one floor of a building

stork storks

a very large bird with long legs and a long straight beak

storm storms

rough weather with wind and rain

a
b
c
d
e
f
g
h
i
j
k
l
m
n
o
p
q
r
s **S**
t
u
v
w
x
y
z

a
b
c
d
e
f
g
h
i
j
k
l
m
n
o
p
q
r
s S
t
u
v
w
x
y
z

story stories

something that is told, usually about things that are not real; fiction

stout

stouter, stoutest

fat

stove stoves

something that produces heat for cooking or heating

straight

straighter, straightest

1 without a bend or turning
2 **straightaway** immediately

strain

strains, straining, strained

1 to pull or try as hard as you can; to try too hard
2 to hurt a muscle

strainer strainers

a tool with small holes for letting liquids through; a sieve

strange

stranger, strangest

unusual; odd

stranger strangers

a person you do not know; a person who does not know the area

strap straps

a long thin piece of leather or material used for fastening things

straw straws

1 the dry stalks of wheat or other grain
2 a thin tube for drinking through

strawberry strawberries

a kind of soft bright red fruit that grows on small plants

stray

strays, straying, strayed

1 to wander away; to get lost
2 an animal that wanders because it has no home

stream streams

anything that is moving steadily (for example, the water in a small river)

street streets

a road with buildings along its sides

strength

how strong someone or something is

stretch

stretches, stretching, stretched

to make longer or wider by pulling

stretcher stretchers

a long piece of material with sticks down two sides, used to carry a person who is ill or has been hurt

strict

stricter, strictest

firm; severe

stride strides

a long pace or step

strike

strikes, striking, struck

1 to hit something hard
2 when workers refuse to work because they believe they are being treated unfairly
3 to refuse to work

string

thin cord used for tying things

strip strips

1 a long narrow piece of something
2 to undress; to uncover

stripes

lots of lines in different colours, making a pattern

stroke

strokes, stroking, stroked

to move your hand gently over something

stroll

strolls, strolling, strolled

to walk along slowly

strong

stronger, strongest

1 able to do difficult things with the body (able to lift heavy things, for example)
2 brave, confident; not easily hurt or damaged

structure structures

1 a building or framework
2 the way something is made up or organised

struggle

struggles, struggling, struggled

1 to fight
2 to try very hard to do something

stubborn

not giving way easily; obstinate

student students

a person who is studying, especially in a college or university

study

studies, studying, studied

1 to learn about something
2 to look at something very closely
3 a room where you study

stuff

stuffs, stuffing, stuffed

1 to fill something very full
2 a substance
3 things that belong to someone

stuffy

stuffier, stuffiest

having little fresh air

stumble

stumbles, stumbling, stumbled

to fall or almost fall, especially by catching your foot on something

stump stumps

1 the part of a tree that is left when the tree has been cut down
2 one of three upright sticks used to bowl at in cricket

stun

stuns, stunning, stunned

1 to amaze or shock someone
2 to strike a person so that he or she is made unconscious

stupid

having no sense; foolish

sturdy

sturdier, sturdiest

strong; well built; healthy

stutter

stutters, stuttering, stuttered

to have difficulty in saying words; to hesitate and repeat words without meaning to; to stammer

a
b
c
d
e
f
g
h
i
j
k
l
m
n
o
p
q
r
s **S**
t
u
v
w
x
y
z

sty sties

1 a place where pigs are kept
2 a small painful swelling on the eyelid

style styles

a way of doing, saying or making something

subject subjects

1 what is being talked about
2 a person who belongs to a country
3 in a sentence, the thing that is doing the action

submarine submarines

a ship that can move along under water

substance substances

something with which things are made; material

subtract

subtracts, subtracting, subtracted

to take one number away from another (−)

succeed

succeeds, succeeding, succeeded

1 to manage to do what you were trying to do; to do well
2 to come after; to follow

suck

sucks, sucking, sucked

1 to take into the mouth by breathing inwards
2 to move something about in your mouth without chewing it (a sweet, for example)

sudden

quick; not expected

suffer

suffers, suffering, suffered

to feel great pain or sorrow

sufficient (say 'suffi**shunt**')

enough; as much as is needed

sugar (say '**shooger**')

a sweet substance made from sugar cane or beet

suggest

suggests, suggesting, suggested

to say what might be done; to hint

suit suits

1 a set of clothes (for example, a jacket with matching trousers or a skirt)
2 to be good or right for; to fit

suitable

just right for a particular purpose

suitcase suitcases

a container with a handle and stiffened sides, used for carrying clothes

sulk

sulks, sulking, sulked

to show that you are in a bad mood by not saying anything

sum sums

1 a problem that you solve using numbers
2 the number you get when you add other numbers together

summer

the warmest season of the year, between spring and autumn

summit summits

the top, especially of a mountain

sun

the large ball of fire in the sky that gives the earth light and heat. The earth goes round the sun once a year.

sunrise sunrises

the time when the sun first appears in the morning

sunset sunsets

the time when the sun goes down at night

supermarket supermarkets

a large shop where people go to buy food and other things

supersonic

faster than the speed of sound

supper suppers

a meal eaten in the evening

supply

supplies, supplying, supplied

1 to provide the things that are needed
2 a quantity or store of things

support

supports, supporting, supported

1 to hold up from underneath
2 to help someone (by giving encouragement, money or advice, for example)
3 to be a fan of a particular sports team (a football team, for example)

suppose

supposes, supposing, supposed

to believe something to be true without knowing for sure

sure

surer, surest

certain; not having any doubt

surf

surfs, surfing, surfed

1 to ride on a special board that floats on the waves
2 to go from one website to another

surface surfaces

the top or outside of something

surgeon surgeons

a doctor who carries out operations

surgery surgeries

a place where doctors or dentists work

surname surnames

the family name; your last name

surprise surprises

1 something nice that you did not expect
2 the good feeling that this gives you

surrender

surrenders, surrendering, surrendered

to give in, especially to an enemy

surround

surrounds, surrounding, surrounded

to be all around

a b c d e f g h i j k l m n o p q r s **S** t u v w x y z

suspect (say 'suspect') suspects

a person who is thought to have done something wrong

suspect (say 'suspect')
suspects, suspecting, suspected

to believe; to have reason to think something (often something bad about a person)

swallow
swallows, swallowing, swallowed

1 to take in through the mouth and throat
2 a kind of small bird with pointed wings and a long forked tail

swamp swamps

soft wet ground; a marsh

swan swans

a large white water bird with a long neck

swap
swaps, swapping, swapped

to give something away and receive something else in return

swarm swarms

a large number of insects moving together

sway
sways, swaying, swayed

to move from side to side

swear
swears, swearing, swore

to use bad words

sweat

liquid that comes through your skin when you are hot

sweatshirt sweatshirts

a type of jumper, usually made of cotton

sweep
sweeps, sweeping, swept

to clean the floor using a broom

sweet
sweeter, sweetest

1 with a pleasant taste like sugar; not sour
2 a small piece of sweet food (for example, a toffee)
3 a dessert; a pudding

sweetcorn

a vegetable with bright yellow seeds that are as tiny as peas

swell
swells, swelling, swelled

to become bigger

swelling swellings

a part that becomes bigger, especially on the body

swerve
swerves, swerving, swerved

to move sideways quickly, especially to avoid something

swift
swifter, swiftest

1 very fast
2 a kind of small bird with long narrow wings

swim
swims, swimming, swam

to move along in water by moving parts of the body

swing swings

1 a moving seat on ropes
2 a ride on a swing
3 to move backwards and forwards when hanging from a fixed point

switch switches

a device for turning on and off electrical or electronic things

sword swords

a metal weapon like a long knife that is sharp on two sides

sycamore sycamores

a kind of tree with large leaves

syllable syllables

a part of a word that has one vowel sound and can be pronounced by itself

symbol symbols

a sign that has a special meaning

sympathy sympathies

a friendly understanding of the feelings or views of another person

synagogue synagogues

a place where Jewish people worship God

synonym synonyms

a word that means the same as another word

system systems

1 a way of putting things in order
2 a group of people or things working together

tT

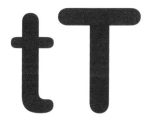

tabby tabbies

1 a cat with greyish or brownish stripes
2 a female cat

table tables

1 a flat piece of furniture that stands on legs
2 a list of numbers or facts in order

tablet tablets

medicine made into a small rounded shape so that it is easy to swallow; a pill

tack tacks

1 a small nail with a large head
2 to fasten things together by using long stitches
3 to change the direction of a sailing boat

tackle

tackles, tackling, tackled

1 to try to do something
2 to try to take the ball from another player (for example, in football)
3 the things that are necessary to do something (for example, fishing tackle)

tadpole tadpoles

a small black water animal with a long tail, which grows into a frog or toad

a
b
c
d
e
f
g
h
i
j
k
l
m
n
o
p
q
r
s

t T

u
v
w
x
y
z

tag tags

1 a label
2 a children's chasing game

tail tails

the part of a creature that sticks out at the back

tailor tailors

a person who makes or alters clothes, especially suits and coats

take

takes, taking, took

1 to get hold of
2 to carry away

tale tales

a story

talent talents

something a person is able to do well; an ability

talk

talks, talking, talked

to speak; to say something

tall

taller, tallest

very high

tame

tamer, tamest

friendly; not wild

tan

1 a light brown colour
2 to make animal skins into leather

tandem tandems

a bicycle for two people

tangerine tangerines

a kind of small sweet orange

tangle tangles

a jumble; a muddle, especially of twisted threads or hair

tank tanks

1 a container made to hold a large amount of liquid or gas
2 a large vehicle that is used in war and is able to move over very rough ground

tanker tankers

a ship or lorry that carries liquids such as petrol or oil

tap taps

1 a knob or handle that is turned to allow liquids to flow
2 a tiny knock

tape tapes

a narrow piece of something (for example, cloth or sticky paper)

taper

tapers, tapering, tapered

to become thin at one end

tapestry tapestries

pictures or patterns made by silk or cotton stitches on heavy cloth

tar

a thick black liquid used to make roads

target targets

something that you aim for

tart tarts

1 a piece of pastry, usually filled with something sweet (jam or fruit, for example)
2 sharp; sour to taste (like a lemon, for example)

tartan tartans

woollen cloth with a pattern of stripes and squares, often used in Scotland for making kilts

task tasks

a piece of work that has to be done; a job

tassel tassels

a hanging bunch of threads often used as a decoration

taste tastes

1 the flavour of food or drink
2 to try a little of some food or drink

tasty

tastier, tastiest

nice to eat; having a nice taste

tax taxes

money that has to be paid to the government by the people

taxi taxis

a car that will take you where you want to go; you pay the driver when you get there

tea

1 a hot drink made from the dried leaves of the tea plant
2 an evening meal

teabag teabags

a small white see-through bag containing tea leaves; you pour boiling water onto it to make tea

teach

teaches, teaching, taught

to help to learn

teacher teachers

a person who teaches

team teams

a number of people who work or play together

tear (say 'teer') tears

a drop of water from the eye

tear (say 'tare')

tears, tearing, tore

to pull apart

tease

teases, teasing, teased

to make fun of

teaspoon teaspoons

a small spoon

teddy teddies

a soft cuddly toy in the shape of a bear

teenager teenagers

a person aged between 13 and 19 years

telephone (phone)
telephones (phones)

an instrument that carries the sound of your voice – usually by wire, using electricity

telescope telescopes

an instrument that you look through to see things that are far away

television (TV) televisions (TVs)

an instrument that makes sound and pictures from waves sent through the air or along a cable

a
b
c
d
e
f
g
h
i
j
k
l
m
n
o
p
q
r
s
t T
u
v
w
x
y
z

a
b
c
d
e
f
g
h
i
j
k
l
m
n
o
p
q
r
s
t T
u
v
w
x
y
z

tell

tells, telling, told

to give news; to say

temper tempers

1 the mood you are in
2 being very angry or annoyed about something

temperature

temperatures

how hot or cold something is

temple temples

a place of worship

tempt

tempts, tempting, tempted

to persuade someone to do something that they would like to do but are trying not to

ten

10; a number

tend

tends, tending, tended

1 to look after
2 to be likely to

tender

1 gentle; kind
2 not tough
3 feeling painful

tennis

a game played by two or four people who use rackets to hit a ball over a net

tent tents

a shelter made of material that is held up by poles and ropes; you use it when camping

term terms

one part of the school year

terminal terminals

1 a place where passengers, vehicles or goods begin or end their journey
2 a computer screen and keyboard linked to a computer which is some distance away

terminus terminuses

the place where a railway or bus route ends

terrace terraces

1 a row of houses joined together
2 a flat area that is above the ground that surrounds it
3 a flat area that is on the side of a hill

terrible

very bad

terrific

very good; excellent

terrify

terrifies, terrifying, terrified

to frighten badly; to fill with fear

territory territories

a large area of land

terror

great fear

test

tests, testing, tested

to try out

tether

tethers, tethering, tethered

to fasten an animal by means of a rope

text

1 written words (in a story, poem or book, for example)
2 a text message that you send or receive using your mobile phone

thank

thanks, thanking, thanked

to say that you are pleased and grateful about something that someone has given you or done for you

thatched

having a roof covering that is made of straw or reeds

thaw

thaws, thawing, thawed

to melt something that was frozen (for example, snow or ice)

theatre theatres

1 a building where plays are acted
2 a room in a hospital where operations take place

theft

stealing; robbery

theme park theme parks

a large area with lots of fairground rides

then

1 coming next
2 at that time

thermometer thermometers

an instrument that measures how hot or cold something is

thick

thicker, thickest

1 wide or deep; not thin
2 with a lot of things close together (trees in a forest, for example)
3 not thin enough to flow easily (used to describe a liquid)

thief thieves

a person who steals; a robber

thigh thighs

the part of the leg between your hip and your knee

thimble thimbles

a hard covering worn on your finger to protect it when you are sewing

thin

thinner, thinnest

1 narrow; not fat
2 able to flow easily (used to describe a liquid)

think

thinks, thinking, thought

to use the mind; to believe

third

1 coming after the second
2 one of three equal parts

thirsty

thirstier, thirstiest

needing or wanting to drink

thirteen

13; a number

thirty

30; a number

a b c d e f g h i j k l m n o p q r s **t T** u v w x y z

a
b
c
d
e
f
g
h
i
j
k
l
m
n
o
p
q
r
s
t T
u
v
w
x
y
z

thistle thistles

a wild plant with prickly leaves and purple flowers

thorn thorns

a prickle or point on a plant stem

thorough

1 taking great care to make sure that everything necessary is done
2 complete

thought thoughts

thinking; an idea in the mind

thousand

1000; a number

thread threads

a very thin line of wool or cotton, used in sewing, knitting or weaving

threat threats

a warning that you mean to harm or punish someone

three

3; a number

thrilling

very exciting

throat throats

the front part of the neck, containing the tubes you use to breathe and swallow

throb throbs

a strong steady beat

throne thrones

a special chair, usually for a king or queen

through

1 from one side to the other; from one end to the other
2 because of

throw

throws, throwing, threw

to release something from your hand and send it through the air

thrush thrushes

a brown bird with a spotted breast

thrust

thrusts, thrusting, thrust

1 to push hard
2 the lifting power of an engine (for example, a rocket)

thud thuds

the noise of something falling or bumping heavily

thumb thumbs

the shortest and thickest finger on your hand

thump thumps

1 a heavy blow, usually made with the fist
2 the dull noise made by a blow of this kind

thunder

the noisy crash that follows lightning

thunderstorm thunderstorms

rough weather with thunder and lightning

tick ticks

1 a mark (✓) used to show that something has been checked or is correct
2 the sound made by a clock or watch

ticket tickets

a card or piece of paper allowing you to enter a special place (such as a cinema, for example) or to travel on a journey by train, plane or bus

tickle

tickles, tickling, tickled

to touch someone lightly with your fingers to make them laugh

tide tides

the daily rising and falling of the sea

tidy

tidier, tidiest

neat; in good order

tie ties

1 a narrow piece of cloth that is sometimes worn round the neck
2 to make a knot

tiger tigers

a large and fierce animal of the cat family with black and orange striped fur

tight

tighter, tightest

fixed or fitting closely together

tights

a piece of clothing worn by girls and women to cover the feet, legs and lower part of the body

tile tiles

a flat piece of baked clay, glass or plastic used with other such pieces to cover roofs, floors or walls

till

1 short for **until**
2 the place where you go to pay in a shop
3 a drawer or box where money is kept in a shop or a bank

tilt

tilts, tilting, tilted

to lean to one side

timber

wood for making things

time

1 the passing of minutes, hours, days, months, years
2 the hour of the day shown on a clock

timid

easily frightened; likely to be afraid; shy

tin

a silvery-white metal

tingle

tingles, tingling, tingled

to have a prickly feeling that may be caused by cold, fear or excitement

tinkle tinkles

a sound like that of a small bell

tinsel

glittering material used for decoration

a
b
c
d
e
f
g
h
i
j
k
l
m
n
o
p
q
r
s
t T
u
v
w
x
y
z

tiny

tinier, tiniest

very small

tip tips

1 the pointed end of something
2 to upset something

tiptoe

tiptoes, tiptoeing, tiptoed

to stand or walk on your toes

tired

needing a rest or a sleep

tissue tissues

1 a piece of soft paper for wiping
2 very thin paper used for wrapping delicate things

title titles

1 the name of a book, a play or a piece of music
2 the first part of a person's name (for example, 'Mrs' or 'Dr')

toad toads

an animal like a large frog with a rough skin

toadstool toadstools

a kind of plant shaped like a small umbrella. Many toadstools are poisonous.

toast

bread made crisp and brown by heat

toaster toasters

an electrical machine for making toast

toboggan toboggans

a light sledge used for sliding on snow for fun, especially down slopes

today

this day

toddler toddlers

a very young child who is just beginning to walk

toe toes

one of the five end parts of the foot

toffee toffees

a sticky sweet made from sugar and butter

together

1 with someone or something
2 at the same time

toilet toilets

1 a large bowl used to get rid of waste matter from the body
2 a room with a toilet

tomato tomatoes

a soft and round red fruit, often eaten in salads

tomb tombs

a grave

tomorrow

the day after today

tone tones

1 the sound of the voice used in speaking or singing; the sound of a musical instrument
2 a shade of colour

tongue tongues

the soft moving part inside your mouth. You use it to taste, eat and speak.

tongue twister tongue twisters

words that are difficult to say together

tonight

this night

tonne tonnes

a large measure of weight, equal to 1000 kilograms

tonsils

the two small lumps at the back of the throat

too

1 also
2 more than enough

tool tools

an instrument that you use to do something with (for example, you use a spoon to mix things)

tooth teeth

one of the hard parts growing out of your jaw, used for biting and chewing

toothache

a pain in a tooth

toothbrush toothbrushes

a small brush that is used to clean teeth

toothpaste toothpastes

a flavoured paste that you put on your toothbrush when you clean your teeth

top tops

1 the highest part
2 a covering or lid for something
3 a piece of clothing worn on the top half of the body
4 a toy that spins

topic topics

something you write, study or talk about

topple

topples, toppling, toppled

to make or become unsteady and fall over

torch torches

an electric light that can be carried

torment (say 'torment')
torments

great pain and suffering

torment (say 'torment')
torments, tormenting, tormented

to cause pain to someone; to tease; to annoy

tortoise tortoises

a slow-moving animal with a hard round shell

torture

tortures, torturing, tortured

to cause great pain to someone on purpose

a b c d e f g h i j k l m n o p q r s t **T** u v w x y z

a b c d e f g h i j k l m n o p q r s t T u v w x y z

toss

tosses, tossing, tossed

to throw into the air

total totals

everything added together; the whole

totter

totters, tottering, tottered

to move unsteadily; to stagger

touch

touches, touching, touched

to feel gently with the hand or another part of the body

tough

tougher, toughest

hard; strong; not easy to cut or bite

tour tours

a journey on which you visit several places

tourist tourists

a person who travels for pleasure

tow

tows, towing, towed

to pull something along using a rope or a chain (for example, a car or a boat)

toward (or towards)

in the direction of

towel towels

a piece of cloth for drying wet things

tower towers

a tall narrow building or part of a building

town towns

a large number of houses and other buildings grouped together

toy toys

something you play with

trace traces

1 a very small amount left behind
2 to copy exactly by following the lines of a drawing through transparent paper
3 to find after searching and following clues

track tracks

1 a path
2 the metal lines on which a train runs
3 a mark left in the ground (by a foot or a tyre, for example)

tracksuit tracksuits

loose trousers and top sometimes worn over sports clothes

tractor tractors

a strong machine for pulling heavy loads

trade

trades, trading, traded

1 to buy and sell
2 a skilled job, especially one in which you use your hands

traffic

movement of vehicles and people

traffic lights

a set of coloured lights (red, orange, green), on a post at a road junction. The lights tell the traffic when to stop or go.

tragedy tragedies

1 a very sad happening
2 a serious play with a sad ending

trail

trails, trailing, trailed

1 to follow a track or the scent of an animal
2 to drag or be dragged behind

trailer trailers

1 a cart or box on wheels, pulled by a car or lorry
2 a short piece of film, made specially to make you interested in seeing the whole film

train trains

1 railway coaches joined to an engine
2 the back part of a dress that trails on the ground
3 to teach someone to do something; to guide

trainer trainers

a kind of shoe, often worn for sports

training

a lesson; a time when you practise something or when someone teaches you how to do something

traitor traitors

a person who tells secrets to the enemy and betrays his or her country

tramp tramps

1 a person with no home or job who wanders around the streets
2 to walk heavily

trample

tramples, trampling, trampled

to walk heavily on, often doing damage

trampoline trampolines

a large frame with springs covered with material on which you can bounce up and down

translate

translates, translating, translated

to change from one language into another

transparent

able to be seen through

transport

transports, transporting, transported

to move things or people from place to place

trap

traps, trapping, trapped

1 to catch in a clever way
2 something specially made to trap an animal or a person

trapeze trapezes

a bar joining two ropes that hang down to make a swing, used in a circus or a gym

travel

travels, travelling, travelled

to move from one place to another

traveller

1 someone who travels
2 someone whose tradition it is to travel around (often in a caravan) instead of living in one place

a
b
c
d
e
f
g
h
i
j
k
l
m
n
o
p
q
r
s
t T
u
v
w
x
y
z

a
b
c
d
e
f
g
h
i
j
k
l
m
n
o
p
q
r
s

t T

u
v
w
x
y
z

tray trays

a flat piece of wood, plastic or metal, used for carrying things

treacle

a dark and sweet sticky liquid made from sugar

treason

the crime of betraying your country

treasure treasures

something very valuable

treasurer treasurers

a person who looks after the money that belongs to a group of people

treat treats

something especially pleasant that you are given (for example, sweets or an outing)

tree trees

a large plant with a trunk, branches and leaves

tremble

trembles, trembling, trembled

to shake with excitement, fear or cold; to shiver

trench trenches

a ditch dug in the earth for a special purpose

trespass

trespasses, trespassing, trespassed

to go into a private place without permission

trial trials

1 a test
2 an examination before a judge to decide whether or not a person is guilty

triangle triangles

1 a flat shape with three straight sides and three corners (▲)
2 a metal musical instrument of this shape, played by striking it with a metal rod

tribe tribes

a group of people ruled by one chief

trick

tricks, tricking, tricked

1 to cheat
2 something clever done either to cheat or to make people smile

trickle trickles

a very small flow of a liquid

tricycle (trike)
tricycles (trikes)

a cycle with three wheels

trifle trifles

1 a small thing of no importance
2 a kind of dessert made of cake, custard, fruit and cream

trigger triggers

a small lever that is pulled to start a machine or to fire a gun

trim

trims, trimming, trimmed

1 to cut and make tidy
2 tidy; neat

trio trios

a group of three people doing something together (for example, singing or playing instruments)

trip trips

1 a journey, especially one for pleasure
2 to stumble and fall

triplets

three people born at the same time to the same mother

triumph triumphs

a great victory or success

trolley trolleys

a small light cart pushed by hand (at the supermarket, for example)

trombone trombones

a long musical instrument made of brass. You play it by blowing.

troop troops

a group of people (for example, soldiers)

tropical

of or like the tropics; very hot

tropics

the part of the world near the equator

trot

trots, trotting, trotted

to move gently with short steps (quicker than walking, slower than running). Horses sometimes trot.

trouble troubles

1 a worry; a problem; a difficulty
2 to worry or to annoy someone

trousers

a piece of clothing for the legs and the lower part of the body

trout trout

a kind of fish that lives in fresh water

trowel trowels

1 a garden tool like a small spade
2 a small flat-bladed tool for spreading cement

truant truants

a person who stays away from school without permission

truck trucks

a vehicle that carries heavy loads

trudge

trudges, trudging, trudged

to walk slowly and heavily as you do when you are tired

true

truer, truest

correct; honest

trumpet trumpets

a musical instrument made of brass that you play by blowing

trunk trunks

1 the thick stem of a tree
2 a large box for carrying things
3 an elephant's long nose

trunks

short trousers worn by men and boys for swimming

trust

trusts, trusting, trusted

to believe that someone is honest

truth

what is true

try

tries, trying, tried

to make an effort to do something

T-shirt T-shirts

a light cotton shirt with short sleeves and no collar

tub tubs

a round container with an open top

tube tubes

1 a thin hollow pipe
2 a soft plastic container from which the contents can be squeezed (for example, toothpaste)
3 the underground railway in London

tuck

tucks, tucking, tucked

to push or put something into or under something else

tuft tufts

a small bunch

tug

tugs, tugging, tugged

1 to pull hard and sharply
2 a small but powerful boat that is used to pull other boats

tulip tulips

a kind of spring flower grown from a bulb

tumble

tumbles, tumbling, tumbled

to fall heavily

tumbler tumblers

a flat-bottomed drinking glass

tummy tummies

short for **stomach**

tuna tuna

a very large fish found in warm seas, used as food

tune tunes

a set of musical notes that sound pleasant together

tunnel tunnels

a covered road or path under the ground (through hills, for example)

turban turbans

a long piece of cloth that some Asian men wrap around their heads

turf

short grass, including its roots and the earth in which it grows

turkey turkeys

a large bird kept on farms

turn

turns, turning, turned

1 to face a different way; to move round
2 to change the direction of travel
3 a chance to do something after other people have had a go

turnip turnips

a root vegetable that is white or yellowish inside

turquoise

1 a greenish-blue precious stone
2 the colour of this stone

turret turrets

a small tower in a building

turtle turtles

an animal with a hard rounded shell that lives mainly in the sea

tusk tusks

a long, slightly curved and pointed tooth found in an animal such as an elephant or a walrus

tweed

a kind of rough woollen cloth (used for suits and heavy coats, for example)

tweezers

a tool with two arms that can be pushed together for getting hold of small things

twelve

12; a number

twenty

20; a number

twice

two times

twig twigs

a very small branch of a tree

twilight

dim light just after sunset

twine

twisted string that is thin but very strong. It is often used in the garden.

twinkle

twinkles, twinkling, twinkled

to shine with small bright flashes

twins

two people born at the same time to the same mother. Some twins are identical.

twirl

twirls, twirling, twirled

to twist round; to spin quickly

twist

twists, twisting, twisted

to turn something (a bottle cap, for example)

twitch

twitches, twitching, twitched

to move suddenly and quickly, usually without meaning to

twittering

chirping sounds, like those made by birds

two

2; a number

type types

1 a special sort; a kind
2 to tap keys on a computer keyboard in order to make words

typhoon typhoons

a great storm

typical

as you would normally expect

tyre tyres

the rubber round the outside of a wheel, often filled with air

a
b
c
d
e
f
g
h
i
j
k
l
m
n
o
p
q
r
s
t
u U
v
w
x
y
z

uU

ugly
uglier, ugliest

not nice to look at

umbrella umbrellas
a folding metal frame covered in waterproof material; you hold it over your head to keep yourself dry when it is raining

umpire umpires
the person who makes sure that a game (cricket or tennis, for example) is played fairly; a referee

uncle uncles
the brother of a father or mother; an aunt's husband

uncommon
unusual

unconscious
not conscious; not knowing what is happening

uncover
uncovers, uncovering, uncovered

to take the lid or covering off something; to reveal

under
1 covered by
2 below; less than

underground
1 under the earth
2 a railway that goes under the ground

undergrowth
the thick plants or grasses that grow under or around trees

underneath
below or under something

underpants (pants)
what you wear underneath your trousers or skirt

understand
understands, understanding, understood

to know what something means

underwear (undies)
clothes worn next to the skin under other clothes

undo
undoes, undoing, undid

1 to untie
2 on a computer, the command that cancels your last instruction

unemployed
having no paid work

unfair
not fair

unfold
unfolds, unfolding, unfolded

to open out something that is folded

unfortunate
having bad luck

unhappy
not happy

unicorn unicorns
an imaginary animal that looks like a horse with one long horn

uniform uniforms

special clothes worn by children who go to the same school or club, or by people who work together (nurses, for example)

union

a joining together

unique

the only one of a kind

unit units

1 one complete thing or set
2 an amount used as a measurement
3 a number under 10

unite

unites, uniting, united

to join together into one

universe

the whole of space and everything that exists, including all the stars and planets

university universities

a place where people may go to learn after leaving school

unkind

not kind or helpful

unless

if not; except if

unload

unloads, unloading, unloaded

to take something off or out of (a lorry or a ship, for example)

unlock

unlocks, unlocking, unlocked

to open with a key

unnecessary

not needed

unpack

unpacks, unpacking, unpacked

to take things out of a case or container

unpleasant

nasty; unkind; not pleasant

untie

unties, untying, untied

to loosen a knot so that both ends of the cord or string are free

until

up to the time of

unwell

ill

up

to a higher place

upon

on; on top of

upper

higher

upright

1 standing straight up; vertical
2 honest and true

uproar

a lot of loud noise and excitement, often caused by anger

upset

upsets, upsetting, upset

1 to make others unhappy
2 to knock over

a
b
c
d
e
f
g
h
i
j
k
l
m
n
o
p
q
r
s
t
u U
v
w
x
y
z

a
b
c
d
e
f
g
h
i
j
k
l
m
n
o
p
q
r
s
t
u
v V
w
x
y
z

upside down

the wrong way up

upstairs

on a higher floor of a building

upwards

up to a higher place

urge

urges, urging, urged

to try to get somebody to do a certain thing

urgent

so important that it needs to be done at once

use (say 'yooz')

uses, using, used

to do something with; to put to some purpose

use (say 'yoos') uses

purpose; usefulness

useful

of some use; helpful

useless

of no use; not useful

usual

often done; happening often

usually

more often than not

utensil utensils

a useful tool, especially in the kitchen

utmost

1 the most that is possible
2 the greatest

vacant

empty

vacuum vacuums

1 a space with no air in it
2 **vacuum cleaner** a machine for lifting dirt (from carpets, for example)
3 **vacuum flask** a container for keeping liquids hot

vague

not certain or clear

vain

vainer, vainest

1 proud; conceited
2 **in vain** uselessly; without any chance of success

valley valleys

low ground between two hills or mountains

valuable

1 very useful
2 worth a lot of money

value values

1 the importance or usefulness of something
2 how much money you would get for something if you sold it

valve valves

an instrument that controls a flow of water, air or electricity

van vans

a vehicle for carrying things

vanilla

a sweet flavouring

vanish

vanishes, vanishing, vanished

to go out of sight; to disappear

vapour vapours

tiny drops of liquid floating in the air as mist, steam or a cloud

variety varieties

1 many different things mixed together
2 a kind

various

of several different kinds

varnish

a substance painted on a surface to make it shiny

vase vases

a container for holding flowers so they can stand in water

vast

very large; of great size

veal

meat from a calf

vegetable vegetables (veg)

a plant grown for food (for example, a carrot or a cabbage)

vegetarian vegetarians

a person who does not eat meat or fish

vehicle vehicles

a machine used for carrying people or things (for example, a car or a van)

veil veils

a thin covering for the face or head, usually to hide it

vein veins

one of the thin tubes that carry blood into your heart

velvet

a kind of cloth that is soft and smooth on one side

verb verbs

a word that says what someone or something does

verdict verdicts

what is decided, especially in a law court

verge verges

the edge of a road or path

vermin

small harmful animals or insects

verse verses

1 a poem
2 one part of a poem

version

one person's description of what has happened; another person's description may be different

versus (v)

against (another team, for example)

vertical

straight up; standing upright; the opposite to horizontal; at right angles to the horizon

vessel vessels

1 a container for liquids
2 a ship

vest vests

a piece of clothing worn next to the skin on the top part of the body, to keep you warm

vet vets

a doctor for animals

vibrate

vibrates, vibrating, vibrated

to shake; to throb

vicar vicars

a priest in the Church of England

vice vices

1 evil; badness
2 a fixed tool that grips things to stop them from moving

vicious

very bad; very wicked

victim victims

a person who has suffered because of what other people have done to him or her or because of illness or an accident

victory victories

when a person or a group of people beats others in battle or in a competition

video videos

moving pictures; a film

video camera
video cameras

a camera that films action and records sound

view views

1 what you can see from where you are
2 what you think about something

vigorous

strong; active

village villages

a number of houses and other buildings grouped together; a small town

villain villains

a wicked person

vine vines

a plant on which grapes grow

vinegar

a sour liquid used for flavouring and for preserving food

violence

1 great force
2 wild and hurtful behaviour towards other people

violet violets

1 a tiny purple flower
2 a purple colour; one of the colours of the rainbow

violin violins

a wooden musical instrument with four strings, held under the chin and played with a bow

virtue virtues

goodness

virus viruses

1 a very small living thing in the blood that often causes illness
2 a program that stops a computer working properly

visible

able to be seen

vision

1 sight
2 something seen in a dream

visit

visits, visiting, visited

to go and see someone or something

vital

necessary for life; very important

vitamin vitamins

a substance living things need in small amounts to help them to stay healthy

vivid

bright and clear

vixen vixens

a female fox

vocabulary

the words used in speaking and writing

voice voices

the sound you make when you speak or sing

volcano volcanoes

a mountain that sometimes throws out melting rock, hot ashes, steam and flames

volleyball

a game in which a ball is thrown back and forward over a net

volume volumes

1 the space something fills
2 a book (often one of several)
3 how loud a sound is

voluntary

done freely and openly, without having been asked to do it and without being paid

volunteer volunteers

a person who offers to do something without being paid

vomit

vomits, vomiting, vomited

to be sick

vote

votes, voting, voted

to make a choice; to choose at an election

vow vows

a solemn promise

vowel vowels

the letters a, e, i, o and u

voyage voyages

a long journey, usually by sea or by spaceship

vulture vultures

a large bird that feeds on dead animals

a
b
c
d
e
f
g
h
i
j
k
l
m
n
o
p
q
r
s
t
u
v **V**
w
x
y
z

a b c d e f g h i j k l m n o p q r s t u v w W x y z

waddle

waddles, waddling, waddled

to walk like a duck

wade

wades, wading, waded

to walk through water or mud

wafer wafers

a very thin biscuit sometimes eaten with ice cream

wag

wags, wagging, wagged

to move something from side to side (your finger, for example)

wage wages

money given for work done

wagon wagons

1 a four-wheeled vehicle that carries heavy loads
2 a railway truck

wail

wails, wailing, wailed

to cry in sorrow

waist waists

the middle of the body, just above the hips

wait

waits, waiting, waited

to stay in a place for a reason

waiter waiters

a man who serves food and drinks in a restaurant or café

waitress waitresses

a woman who serves food and drinks in a restaurant or café

wake

wakes, waking, woke

to stop sleeping

walk

walks, walking, walked

to move on the feet

wall walls

1 the vertical side of a room, joining the floor to the ceiling or the roof
2 a structure made of bricks or stones that divides one piece of land from another

wallet wallets

a small flat case for money or cards, usually carried in the pocket

wallpaper wallpapers

thick paper that covers the walls of a room

walnut walnuts

a kind of nut

walrus walruses

a water animal like a large seal with two long tusks

waltz waltzes

a dance for two people

wand wands

a thin straight stick used by wizards, witches, magicians and fairies, in stories

wander

wanders, wandering, wandered

to move about slowly

want

wants, wanting, wanted

to wish to have

war wars

fighting between countries or large groups of people

ward wards

a hospital room with beds for patients

warden wardens

a person who looks after a building where people live

warder warders

a person who looks after prisoners

wardrobe wardrobes

a cupboard for storing clothes

warehouse warehouses

a large building where goods are stored

warm

warmer, warmest

fairly hot

warn

warns, warning, warned

to tell someone about a possible difficulty or danger that may affect them

wart warts

a small hard lump on the skin

wash

washes, washing, washed

to clean using water

wasp wasps

an insect with black and yellow stripes and a painful sting

waste

1 rubbish
2 to be careless with things; to use more things than you really need

watch watches

1 a small clock, usually worn on the wrist
2 to look at carefully
3 to guard

water

the liquid that is found in rivers and in the sea, and falls as rain

waterfall waterfalls

a stream or river falling from a height

waterproof

made of material through which water cannot go

wave

waves, waving, waved

1 to put one arm up and move your hand quickly from side to side to be friendly
2 a moving line on the surface of water (on the sea or on a lake, for example)
3 one way in which energy sometimes travels

wax

a fatty material that is used to make candles and polish

a
b
c
d
e
f
g
h
i
j
k
l
m
n
o
p
q
r
s
t
u
v
w W
x
y
z

way ways

1 how you do something
2 a road or path

weak

weaker, weakest

not strong

wealthy

wealthier, wealthiest

having a lot of money

weapon weapons

a tool you use to fight or hunt with

wear

wears, wearing, wore

1 to have something on (for example, clothes or jewellery)
2 slight damage caused by a lot of use

weary

wearier, weariest

very tired

weasel weasels

a small and furry wild animal with a long body

weather

how sunny, cold or wet it is outside

weave

weaves, weaving, wove

to make cloth by twisting threads over and under each other

web webs

1 short for **cobweb**
2 another name for the internet

website websites

a place on the internet where you can find or give information

wedding weddings

when two people get married

wedge wedges

a piece of something that is thinner at one end than the other

weed weeds

1 a wild plant that grows where it is not wanted
2 to dig out weeds

week weeks

seven days

weekend weekends

the two days at the end of a week: Saturday and Sunday

weep

weeps, weeping, wept

to cry

weigh

weighs, weighing, weighed

1 to measure how heavy something is
2 to be a certain weight

weight

how heavy something is

weird

weirder, weirdest

very strange

welcome

welcomes, welcoming, welcomed

to be friendly and show you are happy when someone arrives

welfare

good health, comfort, feeling safe

well wells

1 a deep hole holding water or oil
2 in good health
3 in a good way

wellbeing

good health, contentment, feeling safe

wellingtons (wellies)

long rubber boots

west

the direction where the sun goes down

wet

wetter, wettest

having a lot of liquid in it or on it

whale whales

the largest sea animal

wheat

a plant producing grain that is used to make flour

wheel wheels

1 a circle of metal, plastic or wood that turns and helps you to move things more easily
2 to push something that has wheels

wheelbarrow wheelbarrows

a small cart that is pushed along; you use it to carry things (in the garden, for example)

wheelchair wheelchairs

a chair with wheels that is used by people who cannot walk

wheelie bin wheelie bins

a large dustbin on wheels

when

1 a connecting word that refers to a particular time
2 a question word that is used to find out the time at which something happens

while

1 a period of time
2 as long as; during

whimper

whimpers, whimpering, whimpered

to cry softly

whine

whines, whining, whined

1 a long sad cry like the cry of a dog
2 to complain a lot without good reason

whip

whips, whipping, whipped

to stir or beat something (for example, cream) when you are preparing food

whirl

whirls, whirling, whirled

to spin round quickly

whiskers

long stiff hairs on the face (of a cat, for example)

whisper

whispers, whispering, whispered

to speak very quietly

a b c d e f g h i j k l m n o p q r s t u v w **W** x y z

a
b
c
d
e
f
g
h
i
j
k
l
m
n
o
p
q
r
s
t
u
v
w W
x
y
z

whistle whistles

1 a high shrill note made by blowing through the lips or teeth
2 an instrument that you blow into to make a high note

white

1 the colour of clean snow
2 the part of an egg round the yolk

whiteboard

1 a white board that you can write on using pens
2 an electronic screen, like a large computer screen, that several people can work on at the same time

whole

complete; with nothing missing

wick wicks

the string that burns in a candle

wicked

very bad; evil

wicket wickets

1 the three stumps and their bails in cricket
2 the cricket pitch

wide

wider, widest

not narrow

widow widows

a woman whose husband is dead

widower widowers

a man whose wife is dead

wife wives

a married woman

wig wigs

false hair to cover the head

wild

wilder, wildest

1 not tame; fierce
2 not looked after by people
3 out of control

wilderness wildernesses

a wild place where few plants grow and no-one lives

wildlife

wild animals and birds that are not looked after by humans

will wills

1 a written piece of paper saying who is to have a person's things when the person is dead
2 the power to choose what you want to do

willow willows

a kind of tree with thin drooping branches

win

wins, winning, won

to be first or do best in a competition or race

wind (sounds like 'p**inned**')

air that is moving quickly

wind (sounds like 'm**ind**')

winds, winding, wound

to turn round and round

windmill windmills

a building or structure with sails that are turned round and round by the wind

window windows

an opening in the wall of a building that lets light in

wine

a strong drink made from the juice of crushed fruit

wing wings

1 the part of a bird or insect that is used for flying
2 the part of a plane that keeps it in the air

wink

winks, winking, winked

to shut and open one eye while keeping the other eye open. Winking can be one way of sharing a joke or a secret.

winner winners

the person who wins a competition or race

winter

the coldest season of the year, between autumn and spring

wipe

wipes, wiping, wiped

to dry or clean with a cloth

wire wires

thin metal thread

wisdom

being wise

wise

wiser, wisest

clever; understanding a lot

wish

wishes, wishing, wished

1 to want very much, especially something you are unlikely to get
2 what you wish for

wit

cleverness; quickness of mind

witch witches

in stories, a woman who can use magic to do things

wither

withers, withering, withered

to become smaller, drier and paler (usually describes plants)

within

in; inside

witness witnesses

a person who sees something happen

wizard wizards

in stories, a man who can use magic to do things

wobble

wobbles, wobbling, wobbled

to move unsteadily from one side to the other

wolf wolves

a wild animal like a large dog

woman women

an adult female person

wonder

wonders, wondering, wondered

1 to be surprised at
2 to want to know

a
b
c
d
e
f
g
h
i
j
k
l
m
n
o
p
q
r
s
t
u
v

w W

x
y
z

a
b
c
d
e
f
g
h
i
j
k
l
m
n
o
p
q
r
s
t
u
v
w W
x
y
z

wonderful

very good or pleasant; amazing

wood woods

1 a lot of trees growing together
2 the material that trees are made of

wool

1 thread used in weaving or knitting
2 the thick hair on the backs of sheep, lambs and some other animals

woollen

made of wool

word words

1 letters put together so that they mean something when spoken or read
2 a solemn promise

work

something you do; your job

world

1 the planet we live on; the earth
2 everything connected with the life led by a person or a group of people (including friends, activities and places)

worm worms

a long thin animal with a soft body that lives in soil

worn

when something has been used so much that it is of little more use

worry

worries, worrying, worried

to be afraid that something may go wrong

worse

not as good as; less well

worship

worships, worshipping, worshipped

to show that you believe someone to be very good and very important

worth

value

wound wounds

an injury where the skin is cut

When you see the letters 'wr' at the beginning of a word, say 'r'. The 'w' is silent.

wrap

wraps, wrapping, wrapped

to put a covering closely round something

wreath wreaths

leaves or flowers specially made into a ring

wreck

wrecks, wrecking, wrecked

1 to smash completely
2 something that has been smashed (for example, a car or a ship that can no longer be used)

wreckage

the broken pieces of something that has been damaged (in an accident, for example)

wren wrens

a kind of very small brown bird

wrestle

wrestles, wrestling, wrestled

to struggle with a person and try to throw him or her to the ground

wretched

very unhappy or unwell

wriggle

wriggles, wriggling, wriggled

to twist the body about quickly and in an excited way

wring

wrings, wringing, wrung

to twist and squeeze something tightly to get liquid out

wrinkle wrinkles

a line or crease on the skin or in material

wrist wrists

the joint between the hand and the arm

write

writes, writing, wrote

to put words or letters on paper so that they can be read

writhe

writhes, writhing, writhed

to twist and turn your body, usually because something hurts very much

writing

1 something that has been written or printed

2 the special way that you write using a pencil or pen

wrong

not right; not correct

X-ray X-rays

a special photograph of the inside of your body

xylophone xylophones

a musical instrument played by hitting bars of wood or metal with a small hammer

a
b
c
d
e
f
g
h
i
j
k
l
m
n
o
p
q
r
s
t
u
v
w
x X
y
z

a
b
c
d
e
f
g
h
i
j
k
l
m
n
o
p
q
r
s
t
u
v
w
x
y Y
z

yacht yachts

a light sailing boat often used for racing

yam yams

a root vegetable that grows in hot countries

yard yards

1 a measure of length equal to a bit less than one metre
2 a piece of ground next to a building and with a fence or wall around it

yarmulke yarmulkes

a small cap worn on the head by some Jewish men

yawn

yawns, yawning, yawned

to open the mouth and breathe in and out deeply, usually when tired or bored

year years

a period of time equal to 12 months; the time that the earth takes to go once round the sun

yeast

a substance used in baking bread, to make it rise, and also in making beer or wine

yell

yells, yelling, yelled

to shout very loudly

yellow

the colour of a lemon or the yolk of an egg

yesterday

the day before today

yet

1 until now
2 still

yew yews

an evergreen tree with red berries

yield

yields, yielding, yielded

1 to give way; to give in
2 to produce fruit or crops

yogurt (also spelt **yoghourt** or **yoghurt**)

a sour food made from milk, often sweetened with sugar and sometimes flavoured with fruit

yolk yolks

the yellow centre part of an egg

young

younger, youngest

not old

youth

1 the time when you are young
2 a young man

yo-yo yo-yos

a toy that moves up and down a string

zZ

zebra zebras

an African animal like a small horse with black and white stripes

zebra crossing (crossing)
zebra crossings (crossings)

a part of the street specially marked with stripes, for people to cross

zero

the number 0; nothing

zigzag

zigzags, zigzagging, zigzagged

to move sharply to one side and then to the other

zimmer zimmers

a kind of walking frame used by people who find walking difficult

zinc

a whitish metal

zip zips

two lines of metal or plastic teeth that lock so that they keep two pieces of material together (your clothes, for example)

zone zones

a district; an area

zoo zoos

a place where wild animals are kept so that people can look at them

Common words that you should know

a	for	make	the
about	fox	man	their
after	from	me	them
again	get	more	then
all	go	Mr	there
an	going	Mrs	they
and	good	mum	things
are	got	my	think
as	had	new	this
asked	has	no	thought
at	have	not	through
away	he	now	time
back	help	of	to
be	her	off	too
bear	here	oh	took
big	him	old	tree
but	his	on	two
by	home	one	up
called	house	or	us
came	how	other	very
can	I	our	want
can't	I'll	out	wanted
cat	I'm	over	was
children	if	people	water
come	in	play	we
could	into	put	well
dad	is	ran	went
day	it	round	were
did	it's	said	what
didn't	just	saw	when
do	know	school	where
dog	like	see	who
don't	little	she	will
down	long	shouted	with
eat	look	so	would
everyone	looked	some	yes
find	made	take	you
food	magic	that	your

The words in orange can be used as question words. The words which and why can also be used as question words.

Some more useful words

Words to use instead of people's names

I	me	my	mine	myself
you	you	your	yours	yourself, yourselves
he	him	his	his	himself
she	her	her	hers	herself
it	it	its	its	itself
we	us	our	ours	ourselves
they	them	their	theirs	themselves

Words that mean the opposite

awake	asleep	inside	outside
back	front	light	heavy
big	small	loud	quiet
cold	hot	more	less
come	go	near	far
dark	light	new	old
dull	bright	odd	even
easy	difficult	open	closed
float	sink	poor	rich
full	empty	sad	happy
good	bad	under	over
hard	soft	up	down
high	low	wet	dry

Words with similar meanings

afraid	scared	keen	eager
almost	nearly	live	dwell
big	large	lost	missing
centre	middle	loud	noisy
clever	skilful	mend	repair
closed	shut	neat	tidy
crash	collide	silly	foolish
happy	cheerful	start	begin
harm	hurt	sum	total
ill	sick	timid	nervous
jump	leap	wash	clean

Time

Times of day

a.m.	mid-morning	mid-afternoon
daybreak	noon	dusk
dawn	midday	evening
sunrise	p.m.	night
morning	afternoon	midnight

Lengths of time

second	week	year
minute	weekend	decade
hour	fortnight	century
day	month	millennium

Days of the week

Monday	Thursday	Saturday
Tuesday	Friday	Sunday
Wednesday		

Months

1 January	5 May	9 September
2 February	6 June	10 October
3 March	7 July	11 November
4 April	8 August	12 December

Seasons

Spring
(March, April, May)

Summer
(June, July, August)

Autumn
(September, October, November)

Winter
(December, January, February)